Hugh Montefiore is a Jew who
a New Testament scholar in th
Bishop of Birmingham from 197

Also by Hugh Montefiore and published by SPCK/ Triangle:

Confirmation Notebook
A Guide to Christian Belief and Practice
(1968, sixth edition 2004)

Looking Afresh
Soundings in Creative Dissent (2002)

Reaffirming the Church of England
Why it is, What it is and How it is (1995)

The Miracles of Jesus

Hugh Montefiore

First published in Great Britain in 2005 by
Society for Promoting Christian Knowledge
36 Causton Street
London SW1P 4ST

British Library Cataloguing-in-Publication Data
A catalogue record for this book is available from the British Library

ISBN 0-281-05705-2

10 9 8 7 6 5 4 3 2 1

Designed and typeset by Kenneth Burnley, Wirral, Cheshire
Printed in Great Britain by Bookmarque Ltd

Contents

Chapter 1

The Miraculous, the Mythical and the Paranormal

The miracle stories in the Gospels can be properly understood only in the light of their theology (Richardson, 1941: pp. 38f.). But this does not preclude the study of their historical origins, even though this may produce probabilities rather than certainties. There are miracle stories in the Gospels which are usually thought to have their historical origin either in divine miracles carried out by Jesus or in tales moulded to convey his spiritual message. The object of this book is not to quarrel in some cases with either of these explanations, but to explore the possibility that most passages may best be explained in neither of these two ways, but rather as paranormal phenomena.

The exploration falls into five parts:

1   A consideration of what is meant by the three categories of possible explanation – a miracle, a tale moulded to convey a spiritual message and a paranormal occurrence.
2   A short account of the study of parapsychology to establish its credentials.
3   An inquiry into the criteria to be used in judging probabilities of historical authenticity in general, and in particular of any paranormal phenomena in the Gospels.
4   A commentary on those passages in the Gospels which may be thought to fall into this category.

5   An appraisal of what conclusions, if any, may be drawn from this study.

As for miracle, there are several meanings which may be given to the word. Its Latin origin suggests that it means merely 'something to be wondered at' and it is sometimes used in this sense today: 'It was a miracle that the car missed hitting me by a bare inch', someone might say, meaning that the near miss was a matter of amazement and wonder (and thankfulness).

The more common meaning of miracle refers to events which violate the accepted order of nature, whether this order is understood as deterministic, in the Newtonian sense of certain causes always having the same effects, or as statistical, as quantum theory requires, in the sense that there is a certain indeterminacy in nature. Some things, however, are statistically exceedingly improbable, even if they are possible, and any such events are accepted as producing a violation of the accepted natural order quite as much as they would be under the old Newtonian model. In either case such events may be regarded as miracles.

There are those who reject all miracles because they do not believe that the uniformity of nature has been violated. Hume, for example, held that the apparent laws of nature are in fact only universally observed uniformities, and a miracle would imply that such uniformities are not in fact universal. Any event which appeared to breach this universality could be credible only if the evidence in favour of its occurrence is greater than the general expectation in favour of uniformity. Since Hume did not consider that this has ever been the case, he held that miracles do not occur, although the possibility of their occurrence is not entirely ruled out (Hume, 1894: Section 10).

An attitude to nature based upon order in the universe originates from Greek tradition, which regained prominence in more modern times from the Enlightenment onwards. It has even reached the point where some deny there are any special acts of God:

> Such a view is not deistic in the pejorative sense, in that it allows for a continuing relationship of God to the world as source of existence and giver of purpose to the whole. It is deistic in so far as it refrains from claiming any effective causation on the part of God in relation to particular occurrences. (Wiles, 1974: p. 36)

Those who believe that it is not possible to breach the order of nature are forced to find other explanations for the existence of miracle stories in the Gospels. They have held that miraculous stories in the Gospels have developed partly to illustrate the power of Jesus and partly to embody spiritual truths of Christ's teaching. Such was the view of the nineteenth-century Tübingen school of New Testament criticism. Thus about Baur: 'He discerned in the [Gospel] narratives a mixture of real occurrences where such were possible on naturalistic grounds, legends or myths springing up out of the fertile soil of faith, inventions as is the case of most of John's miracles' (Bruce, 1890: p. 94). It has been held that 'the miraculous element does not belong to the original events but to the later interpretation of them. It is not fact, but fiction' (Thompson, 1911: p. 209).

Gospel miracles have also been explained as midrash, stories not intended to be literally true but told to disclose the meaning of Jesus' ministry, and often showing how Old Testament events were fulfilled in Jesus.

> Did Jesus intend to feed the multitude with loaves and fishes, or is that a retelling of the story of God feeding the chosen people in the wilderness with manna? Was the raising of the widow's son at Nain an event of history or a retelling of the

story of Elijah raising the widow's son? Does the fourth gospel perpetuate the midrash tradition by turning the Lucan parable about Jesus and the rich man into a historical narrative that asserted that Lazarus had been raised from the dead? (Spong, 1992: p. 20)

Those who have been influenced by the Enlightenment have not all dispensed with the idea of miracles. There have been attempts made to combine both the Greek view of the order of nature and the Judaeo-Christian view of God's almighty power in a way that still finds a place for them:

Constancy of purpose is a noble characteristic. It shows itself, not in unalterable uniformity of conduct, but in perpetual self-adaptation, with an infinite delicacy of graduation, to different circumstances, so that, however these may vary, the one unchanging purpose is always served . . . If we adopt this view, we will have to hold that no Law of Nature as discovered by physical science is ultimate . . . No doubt it is true that the same cause will always produce the same effect in the same circumstances. Our contention is that an element in every actual cause, and indeed the predominant element, is the active purpose of God fulfilling itself with that perfect constancy that calls for an infinite graduation of adjustments in the process. Where any adjustment is so considerable as to attract attention, it is called a miracle. (Temple, 1934: p. 267)

If this view be accepted, it does not necessarily follow that every apparent violation of the natural order is to be attributed to the direct intervention of God. A miracle could take place by someone acting in the name and power of God. Miracles attributed to Jesus in the Gospels are of this character. There could also be other causes, such as supernatural entities other than God, either divine or satanic, which might be responsible for such breaches of the natural order.

It seems clear that when a miracle is claimed, it refers to an event or phenomenon which is beyond the power of human beings to effect unaided. But it is not equally clear precisely what are the exact limits to the powers of humankind. As Professor G. F. Woods reminded us:

Do we really know the full potentialities of the natural world? Can we be sure that the future will not disclose a series of natural powers which are at present unknown to us? I do not see how we can be sure that we know the limits of human power, or the limits of what we call the natural order. Even so, as a matter of common sense, we do accept general standards of natural probability which we trust in the everyday business of keeping alive. We do not really expect that a steamship will ever fly. But there is a real distinction between accepting the general stability of nature as a fact and affirming that we know precisely the limits of its potentialities. (Woods, 1965: p. 24)

It is the contention of those who accept the paranormal that, far from knowing the limits of human potentialities, we have to accept that there are powers, whether latent in all persons or given to certain individuals, which far exceed normal human limits, and that little is known at present about the origin and nature of these powers.

What, then, is the paranormal? It is the occurrence of phenomena which appear to breach the order of nature, but which cannot be regarded as specially caused by God, because such phenomena often take place seemingly without point or purpose. They just happen. Parapsychology, in the words of the founders of the Society for Psychical Research, concerns 'those faculties of man, real or supposed, that appear to be inexplicable on any generally recognised hypothesis'.

There are roughly three categories of phenomena that go to make up the study of parapsychology; first the familiar spontaneous incidents that crop up unbidden and unexpected in everyday life, e.g. premonitions, telepathic messages, crisis apparitions, hauntings, poltergeists, etc., secondly effects that are elicited intentionally in the laboratory, be they extrasensory or extramotor, thirdly a mixed category of phenomena, associated with specially gifted individuals which can hopefully be observed under more or less controlled conditions, albeit in a form, or at a time, that can never be precisely specified in advance. (Beloff, 1993: p. xi)

This study is concerned with the first class of events, that is, phenomena that crop up unexpectedly. These might be divinely inspired breaches of the natural order. Such interventions are not absolutely to be ruled out during the ministry of Jesus, if only because the incarnation itself was just such a divine intervention. But when a so-called 'Gospel miracle' falls into a category of phenomena not only found in the Gospels but also parallelled in everyday life in situations where it lacks any special significance, some other explanation seems to be needed. It may rightly be considered a paranormal rather than a supernatural phenomenon.

I will not discuss every 'miraculous' event recorded in the Gospels. I will not deal with those connected with the birth of Jesus, for I have already dealt with these elsewhere (Montefiore, 1992). Readers will find no mention here of the stilling of the storm on the Lake of Galilee (Matthew 8.23–7; Mark 4.35–41; Luke 8.22–5), the raising of the widow's son at Nain (Luke 7.11–17), the coin in the fish's mouth (Matthew 17.23–7), or the cursing of the fig tree (Matthew 21.18f.; Mark 11.12–14). This is because I am not convinced that these stories interpret accurately what actually took place: they do not fall into known categories of paranormal phenomena and I am disinclined to believe that they are the result of divine interventions in the natural order. However, other 'miracles' of Jesus' public ministry that are susceptible to a paranormal explanation are the subject of this study and we will consider the relevant texts in some detail.

Chapter 2

Beyond the Natural Order

The serious scientific study of events which breach the natural order did not start until the nineteenth century. It began as a kind of reaction to the mechanistic and reductionist theories of the natural sciences which stemmed from the Enlightenment, and which Newtonian physics and the Darwinian theory of evolution had made popular. Its proponents aligned themselves with scientists in as much as they were willing both to experiment, to question received opinion and to present their work for open debate.

The study of parapsychology was preceded by mesmerism, in so much as the latter involved persons who in a somnambulist state experienced extrasensory perception, in particular clairvoyance. Then spiritualism raised the question of survival after death. Foremost among its practitioners was D. D. Hume (1833–86), the best-known medium of all time and, if witnesses are to be believed, a man of a most extraordinary range of paranormal gifts. He and others were investigated by distinguished scientists (including Crookes, later to be President of the Royal Society), but séances (which might include materializations) were privately arranged and dismissed by a sceptical public. Despite scandals caused by fraudulent mediums, some outstanding mediums offered themselves for public investigation, in particular 'mental' rather than 'physical' mediums who allegedly were the mouthpieces of discarnate entities. Survival research reached its zenith with the so-called 'cross correspondences', lasting from 1901 to the 1930s, in which prominent people through automatic writing produced references to classical literature, allegedly sent by other prominent people who had died, in such a way that they only made sense when collated.

In 1882 the Society for Psychical Research (SPR) was founded. Its purpose was to study paranormal phenomena 'without prejudice or prepossession and in a scientific spirit'. Its members were dedicated people who were cautious in their conclusions. Its first President was Henry Sidgwick, Professor of Moral Philosophy at Cambridge. Within five years no fewer than eight Fellows of the Royal Society served on its Council; one of its Presidents included a future Prime Minister, Arthur Balfour; and Gladstone, Tennyson and Ruskin were among its honorary members.

The work of the SPR included the full range of 'psychic' phenomena. There was a committee on thought transference, defined as 'any influence which may be exerted by one mind upon another, other than any generally recognized means of perception' (i.e. extrasensory perception). There was also a committee on mesmerism which was to look into the effects of hypnotism. The committee on physical phenomena included dowsing in its remit. Mediums were also included, but the SPR was suspicious of them, and was more interested in the implications of psychic phenomena for gainsaying materialism than for proving survival after death. There were two committees concerned with 'spontaneous' phenomena; one on haunted houses dealt with phenomena in particular places, especially apparitions; while the literary committee was concerned with phenomena focused on persons, such as premonitory dreams, 'second sight', spontaneous telepathic phenomena and apparitions seen close to the time of a person's death, which was unknown to the experient.

Within four years of its foundation, the SPR had published its *magnum opus*, a two-volume work entitled *Phantasms of the Living* (Gurney et al., 1889), citing 702 cases submitted to the Society 'dealing with all cases where there is reason to suppose that the mind of one human being has affected the mind of another, without speech uttered or word written or sign made'. Most of these were alleged cases of telepathy, both spontaneous and experimental; there were also alleged apparitions of the living (among which 'crisis apparitions' of the dying were included, provided that these occurred within twelve hours of death). The authors did not claim from all this proof of the paranormal, and admitted the lack of sufficient evidence in most spontaneous cases of telepathy. Particularly striking were thirteen well-evidenced 'crisis apparitions', although the authors could not exclude the possibility of what Beloff has called 'chance expectation', even though the odds on this seemed extremely high.

The SPR has amassed over the years massive archives, few of which have been made public, but a selection was published in the centenary year of the Society (Mackenzie, 1982). From 1882 onwards the Society published its *Proceedings*, although the founding fathers did not confine their writing to this. For example, an important volume of Frederic Myers was published after his death in 1903. *Proceedings* was superseded by *The Journal of the Society for Psychical Research*, which continues today. (The latest issue of the *Journal*, as I write this chapter, contains an account of how a medium assisted the police in discovering the identity of a murderer, giving evidence for which the authors of the account can see no feasible explanation other than genuine messages from the murdered woman herself.) In addition to the *Journal*, the Society also produces regularly a less academic publication.

Meanwhile, psychical research began to flourish outside Britain, both among individuals and in particular through organizations such as the American Society for Psychical Research, set up in 1895, and the French Institut Metapsychique Internationale, founded in 1919. In 1921 an International Congress on Psychical Research was held in Denmark and repeated later in Poland and France. This was a time when clairvoyants and mediums flourished. They provoked controversy and criticism and sometimes were shown to be fraudulent. Among the most remarkable was the Italian Eusapia Palladino, flamboyant and fantastic, who nevertheless impressed even the sceptical.

Psychological research took a new turn at Duke University in the USA under the leadership of J. B. Rhine (1895–1980). There had been experimental work in card-guessing before Rhine but he benefited from advances in statistical analysis and introduced a revolutionary rigorism into the study of psychical phenomena. Special cards were designed with distinctive and easily remembered symbols. His early work showed astonishing results in successful card-guessing, although later experimentation did not produce such consistency. Evidence of precognition was also produced by this means. Rhine was determined to show that extrasensory perception takes place, and that it could be made scientifically respectable. He concentrated on experimental rather than spontaneous phenomena, thus inaugurating the more modern tendency of psychical research for 'clinical' or laboratory experimentation. Despite this scientific approach, parapsychology has by and large lost the interest of most scientists which it had gained in the 1890s; today there is only one Fellow of the Royal Society associated with psychical research. Chairs in Utrecht and Hamburg have been closed down, and the only chair in parapsychology in Europe today is the Koestler chair in Edinburgh.

Nevertheless, recent developments have gained ground, including Kirlian photography, said to show non-material energies in the human body, and so-called 'free response ESP', in which the target is not something which requires a 'right or wrong' answer (like a card), but a more general response, so that the percipient's success in guessing it is judged by a range of points. There has been research too into the possibility of extrasensory perception in dreams. To produce a relaxed and sensually deprived state more receptive to ESP, the *ganzfeld* has been developed:

> The simplest way of producing the effect is to make the subject wear translucent goggles through which light can be shone. To complete the absence of perceptual patterning, earphones should be worn into which a white noise (something like the sushing sound of waves breaking) can be fed while, to obviate tactile and somatic sensations, the body should be relaxed and cocooned with ample cushioning. (Beloff, 1993: p. 166)

Other developments include examination of the 'electronic voice phenomenon', according to which voices from discarnate entities are said to appear on electronic tapes (Raudive, 1971), and of near-death experiences, in which a similar pattern of experiences has been observed among people very close to death, even clinically dead, but who have subsequently recovered (Parnia et al., 2001), while scholarly research into alleged former lives among children aged three to eight years has produced remarkable results (Stevenson, 1987; 2003).

I am much indebted to J. Beloff (1993) for this much-abbreviated survey of parapsychology over the last century and a half. It has been given in the hope that the reader will recognize that parapsychology is worth taking seriously. It is still ridiculed by well-known scientists with an acknowledged bias against the non-material, such as Richard Dawkins when he writes: 'paranormalism could be called an abuse of the legitimate sense of poetic wonder which true science should be feeding' (Dawkins, 1998: p. xi). Nevertheless the more open-minded would admit that the phenomena which it studies appear to be inexplicable by any generally recognized hypothesis.

Such hypotheses do exist. Sheldrake (2003: pp. 268ff.) lists several of them. It has been suggested that paranormal phenomena can be explained by extra dimensions of existence other than those of time and space. Some contend that they are the result of a kind of resonance between similar patterns of nervous activity. Quantum physics has been held to provide definitive explanation. Sheldrake has his own theory of 'morphic fields'. When discussing healing phenomena, in Chapter 11, I point out alterations in Matthew Manning's EEG spectrum which took place, as though there could be some unknown and as yet unmeasurable radiation; and when considering in Chapter 7 the bright shining of Jesus at his transfiguration, I suggest a possible psychosomatic explanation (as also in levitation, *incendium amoris* and the 'odour of sanctity'). None of these theories, however, covers the whole field, and they show how far we are from understanding these unexplained phenomena.

Parapsychologists have studiously restricted their interest to secular phenomena. This means that, despite the wide range of their interests, there remain some allegedly paranormal phenomena which have not been investigated. I refer to phenomena observed among saints and mystics, some of which are also recounted in the Gospels with reference to Jesus. In so far as they are (in the case of saints) often attested by sworn statements of priests and religious, they can be said to have stronger testimony than many phenomena studied by parapsychologists. Fortunately, many instances of such allegedly paranormal phenomena have been collected and rigorously examined by Fr Herbert Thurston (1952), upon whose work I have drawn heavily in the chapters devoted to these subjects.

Chapter 3

Criteria

I used to be a lecturer in the New Testament in the University of Cambridge, and I remember my position on some of the miracles and other mysterious events in the Gospels. I tended to vacillate. I thought that they were legends, symbolic expressions of the spiritual ministry of Jesus or myths and stories that came into existence after his death, often modelled on Old Testament prototypes, rather like some of the stranger material of the apocryphal gospels. But I was haunted by the thought that they were supernatural events, either caused by the direct intervention of God or wrought through the divine nature of Jesus. It never occurred to me that there might be something paranormal about them, and indeed I would have been laughed out of court by my fellow lecturers and professors had I suggested this. Such an attitude might have betrayed ignorance about the paranormal, especially as manifested in the lives of Christian mystics, or perhaps because some may share the Enlightenment position that such matters were purely superstitious.

However, my views began to change. I became interested in the paranormal and I have lately written a survey of the whole field of paranormal phenomena (Montefiore, 2002). As a young man I was interested in the Christian mystics and read quite a lot about them. Half a century ago I bought a book by Fr Herbert Thurston called *The Physical Phenomena of Mysticism* (1952), mentioned in the previous chapter. It dealt with some of the more perplexing characteristics of mysticism. Its author was a very learned but somewhat sceptical Jesuit who would let nothing through unless it had been thoroughly researched and rigorously tested. Among its seventeen chapters are studies of the Luminous Phenomena of Mysticism, Seeing without Eyes, Multiplication of Food, and the Mystic as Hunger Striker, as well as subjects such as levitation, stigmata and bodily incorruption. The phenomena with which it deals are patently paranormal. Fr Thurston's book demonstrates a mysterious link between mystics, saints and the paranormal. I was struck by the fact that the mystics did not want these curious manifestations to be generally known: St Teresa of Avila, for example, prayed to God that she would experience no more levitation.

Since those early days my life has been taken up with other matters and Thurston's book remained untouched on my shelves for many years. I read it again in connection with another book I was writing, and on rereading it a thought crossed my mind: if there is a connection between holiness and the paranormal, might we find this also in the Gospel stories? Since these paranormal phenomena in no way impaired the holiness of the saints and mystics among whom they appeared, the same would be true if Jesus had paranormal powers. I was struck by the way in which the Gospels repeatedly show Jesus asking his disciples or those whom he had healed to keep quiet and not to tell others, in the same kind of way in which the mystics were reluctant to talk about strange phenomena in their lives. Perhaps his reasons were similar, rather than simply a desire to keep his Messiahship a secret. I thought it worthwhile investigating the Gospels to see what I could find. This book is the result of my exploration.

Exploring the possibility that Jesus had paranormal powers is quite different from considering whether he was a magician, as some have alleged. Magic is the manipulation of the powers of nature for one's own ends. There is no hint that Jesus practised spells and manipulated people and things. It has been claimed, from an obscure passage in Rabbinic writings (which on the few occasions when Jesus is mentioned are generally hostile to him) that he learnt magical arts in Egypt (B. Yoma 66b). But if Jesus ever did go to Egypt, the only occasion would have been as a baby when the Holy Family fled to escape from the clutches of Herod (Matthew 2.14ff.). The theory that Jesus was a magician is largely based on the magical papyri of ancient Egypt. The fact that the exponent of this theory regards Jesus' greatest example of magic to be the Eucharist, which is called 'a simple report of a familiar magical operation – giving enchanted food to cause love' (Smith, 1985: p. 122) hardly increases respect for this view. As Meier (1991: vol. 2, pp. 545ff.) has pointed out, Jesus' miracles normally arise from interpersonal relationships, in which a person in need makes a request: Jesus' verbal response is terse and the mighty works depend on his personal will. His action does not hurt or punish anyone. Jesus' ministry is carried out in obedience to his Father's will and in fulfilment of Old Testament prophecy; his mighty works symbolize the partial realization of the kingdom of God. His was a spiritual ministry, not carried out for personal gain but in accordance with divine authority. By contrast, magic brings essentially trivial benefits in which each case is discrete. Nonsense formulae may be used, and there is a technical manipulation of various allegedly supernatural forces.

A more serious suggestion is that Jesus' ability to work wonders comes from a contemporary Jewish tradition. It has been claimed that Jesus should be seen as part of first-century charismatic Judaism, possibly a Galilean phenomenon (Vermes, 1983: p. 69). But the fact that only four members of this tradition can be named (Honi, his two grandsons and Hanna) is hardly firm evidence that there existed a movement of this kind of which Jesus was a member. At the same time, it may well have been that they shared with Jesus some paranormal gifts which enabled them to carry out the deeds attributed to them in Rabbinic tradition. Nor are paranormal gifts to be confined to these charismatic Jews of the first century; others in the ancient world are reported to have had special gifts of healing. Simon Magus, who was said to have practised sorcery in Samaria, was one of these until he heard the good news of the Gospel and was baptized (Acts 8.13). Another person roughly contemporary with Jesus was Apollonius of Tyana who, according to Philostratus, also had remarkable powers of healing. But Jesus' ministry was pre-eminently a spiritual one. Even if it was through healings that he attracted attention in the short period of his public ministry, these were performed out of compassion for the sufferers and to fulfil Old Testament prophecies of the Messiah, not to earn him a living. Far from being a magician, he used his powers not for his own gain, but in the service of God.

The view that Jesus' mighty acts were all a result of the intervention of God is one to be taken seriously although there are serious difficulties here. It would seem that God interferes very rarely in the world (some would even hold that he never does so at all) and it is difficult to believe that God intervened so often in the ministry of Jesus if intervention only very rarely occurs elsewhere. If Jesus fed five thousand in the wilderness through the direct intervention of God, why has not God fed millions of people who have died of starvation in far more desperate conditions? There is even a christological problem: 'He had to be made like his brethren in every respect', we read (Hebrews 2.17) – he worked, slept, was angry, wept. His teaching and ministry were inspired throughout by the Holy Spirit, but it seems inconsistent with this humanity that he should have used divine power to intervene directly in the affairs of this world.

I have here been making some assumptions about the historicity of the Gospels, a historicity severely questioned in the last two hundred years of New Testament criticism. To what extent can they be regarded as containing reliable historical information of the earthly ministry of Jesus? The Gospels were not written primarily as historical records but to proclaim the good news of Christ. There are those who regard everything in the Scriptures as true, even though this claim is not made in the Scriptures themselves, and it must therefore be regarded as a dogma derived from tradition. There are others who believe that, apart from the facts that Jesus lived, taught and died, there is no reliable history in the Gospels; and what is found there is read back from the Christ of faith rather than from the Jesus of history. The fact that there are considerable differences between the three Synoptic Gospels (as well as considerable agreements) shows how free writers were to make creative changes to the traditions that they had inherited; and the Fourth Gospel shows the extent to which these traditions diverged even in those early days. Clearly, if the Scriptures are subjected to intelligent criticism, no absolute historical certainties can be obtained from the Gospels. Some things can have such a high degree of probability, however, that they can be regarded as practically certain.

What criteria should be used in the search for historical probability? Generally speaking, a saying or story of or about Jesus should be accepted as authentic history when there is no good reason for rejecting it per se. As for specific criteria, those enumerated by Meier (1991: vol. 2, pp. 161–95) should be followed: any passage that causes embarrassment and is therefore softened and changed in other Gospels is likely to be authentic; any action or saying of Jesus which is not consonant with the Judaism of his day is likely to be authentic (though it is ridiculous to reject any saying as inauthentic because it is consonant with the Judaism of his day, for as a Jew Jesus never rejected his Jewish inheritance); any action or saying that is coherent with others in the Gospels or can be shown to have led to his crucifixion is also most probably authentic. Most important of all is multiple attestation: any saying or story which appears in at least two separate traditions is most likely to be based on what Jesus said or did.

There are further criteria. Sayings or stories bearing traces of Aramaic, the language that Jesus actually spoke, are likely to be authentic (and also I believe sayings which can be translated back into Aramaic poetry). So also details of Palestine that can be identified. Vividness is an ambiguous criterion: it may be the result of personal memories but, on the other hand, there are vivid passages in the Fourth Gospel which are likely to have been the product of the author's imaginative and creative powers. Those passages which accord with the tendencies of a developing Synoptic tradition should be treated with suspicion. Finally there is, as I have indicated above, the criterion of historical presumption: a saying or story is likely to be authentic unless there are good reasons for thinking otherwise. These are the criteria, then, which will be used in the passages which follow.

Moving from criteria for assessing the historical authenticity of the Gospels, there remain to be decided criteria to evaluate the probability that a particular passage contains a genuine record of paranormal phenomena. Professor R. Morris (2000: p. 110), the Koestler Professor of Parapsychology at Edinburgh University, has suggested that the following questions be asked of any allegedly paranormal phenomenon or activity:

- Is it best described as a coincidence?
- Is it the result of poor observation?
- Have observations about it been misinterpreted?
- Is there an as yet unknown natural cause?
- Is there a hidden natural cause?
- Is it the result of self-deception?
- Has there been deception or self-deception by others?
- Has there been a distorted impression through biological or intellectual malfunction?

In the case of events or sayings originating nearly two thousand years ago, it is impossible to answer any of these questions with certainty. One can only hazard possibilities or probabilities. Furthermore, when dealing with sayings or events contained in literature, I suggest that the following questions also be asked:

1   What is the general credibility of the witnesses to an alleged paranormal event or activity? Was anyone else present when it took place? How reliable in general is the person to whom it occurred? How rigorous have been inquiries into these matters during the lifetime of the persons concerned?

2   How much time has intervened between what happened and its first written account? Are any exaggerations likely to have occurred during the intervening period?

3   Is the account of what happened internally coherent? If there are any inconsistencies, are they likely to have been caused by the blurring of memories?

4   Is the phenomenon or activity unique or are there any other similar examples which are well attested?

5   How strong are the general arguments against this type of happening?

6   What is the balance of probability between accepting it as paranormal and looking for some (as yet unknown) natural explanation?

These questions should be asked whether a supernatural or paranormal explanation is sought. Some of them (e.g. question 2) apply to all the passages under investigation. Most of them can only be answered in terms of probability. In dealing with the passages in the chapters that follow I have not attempted to apply each and every question. I am concerned here only with asking questions concerning the paranormal.

Chapter 4

Awareness at a Distance: Telepathy

Jesus showed great powers of insight and intuition. But he also seems to have been able to know things which were happening at a distance. Telepathy involves the transfer of knowledge between two people without any auditory or visual or any other natural form of communication. It happens unconsciously. It is perhaps the most common of all paranormal gifts, and many people believe that they have experienced it at some time in their lives. Serious exploration began with the foundation of the Society for Psychical Research in 1882. A past President of the Society wrote in 1947:

> The Society for Psychical Research has made a collection of such cases extending over more than half a century. Each case has been carefully scrutinised before publication, the first-hand account of the principal witness and the corroboration of other witnesses has been obtained, letters and contemporary documents examined, obituary notices checked and in many cases witnesses personally interviewed. The number of cases passed as reliable runs into hundreds. Many more have been filed but not published on account of some evidential defect. No one who really wishes to know the truth about telepathy can ignore these cases, which are recorded in the *Proceedings* and *Journal* of the above named society. (Tyrrell, 1947: pp. 52f.)

Since then J. B. Rhine at Duke University in the USA has carried out tests for extrasensory perception, using card-guessing techniques. Further extensive tests have been made under strict experimental conditions, including the *ganzfeld*, in which one person is asked to identify the drawing or message that another person is sending. Twentieth-century experiments demonstrated successes beyond those which would be expected through random probability. In the more recent past there have been further successful advances in researching telepathy, both between humans and with animals. After recounting these, Sheldrake (2003: p. 81) sums up conclusions as follows:

1 Telepathy is a natural, not a supernatural, phenomenon.
2 Telepathic influences can come to consciousness when dreaming, waking or fully awake.
3 It generally occurs between people who are closely bonded.
4 The most striking cases involve death, distress, accident or other emergencies.
5 Usually one person takes an active role in telepathic communication.

Sheldrake goes on to recount his own experimental research into telephone telepathy. Subjects were chosen who had had telepathic experience. They were told to expect telephone calls at certain times, which would come from one of four possible callers. They had to guess who was calling them, naming the caller before he or she could speak. Video-cameras were used against possible cheating or errors. Those who were just guessing could be expected to be right 25 per cent of the time. Out of 854 such texts, with 65 different subjects, the average success rate was 42 per cent, 'which was astronomically significant statistically, with odds against chance 10^{26} to one' (Sheldrake, 2003: p. 104).

Thus the evidence for telepathy is very strong indeed.

We turn next to examine cases where this may occur in the Scriptures.

Telepathy is occasionally found in the Old Testament. Samuel, for example, knew the location of Saul's lost asses (1 Samuel 9.20) and Elijah is credited with these strange powers. He is said to have warned Israel's king not to approach certain places, as the king of Syria's men would be there to destroy him. This happened two or three times and the king avoided the danger. This so annoyed the king of Syria that he believed one of his own staff was betraying him. But his servants denied this, and reported to him that Elijah the prophet in Israel told the king of Israel the words that he spoke in his bedchamber (2 Kings 6.8–12). These stories refer to far-off events and there is inevitably much doubt about their provenance and date; doubtless they were told in oral tradition before they were written down. But they are strange stories to have been made up and no certainty can be reached about their historicity. Nevertheless they are evidence that telepathy was believed to exist in Old Testament times.

In the light of this, we can examine some Gospel passages.

The healing of a paralytic man (Mark 2.1–12; Matthew 9.1–8; Luke 5.17–20)

Matthew and Mark both locate this healing in Capernaum (Matthew calls it 'his own town' because Capernaum was Jesus' headquarters for his Galilean mission), while Luke is vague on both place and time ('And it came to pass on a certain day'). The similarity of the three accounts suggests that they derive from a single source. It seems likely that Matthew and Luke have derived their accounts from Mark. Matthew's is the shorter account, but then he often shortened Marcan accounts (although a minority of scholars hold that Mark lengthened Matthean stories); while Luke seems to exaggerate ('and there were Pharisees and teachers of the Law sitting by, who had come from *every* village of Galilee and Judaea and from Jerusalem . . .').

Jesus healed the man of his paralysis. Nevertheless there are problems about the story as it stands. Did Jesus so early in his ministry claim as Son of Man the power to forgive sins? Some would say that Jesus was not claiming to be *the* Son of Man, but only intended by the phrase humankind in general. But he could hardly have meant that anyone has power to forgive sins, since this was the prerogative of God. The story is told as a sign of Jesus' Messianic power and authority. But elsewhere Jesus refused to give a sign, and his other healings seem to have been carried out from compassion, and to fulfil Old Testament prophesies of the Messianic age (Rawlinson, 1949: p. 24). For this reason it has been suggested that the conflict with the scribes and Pharisees has been added later to a straightforward tale of healing. This, however, does not take into account the possibility that Jesus was not always consistent, acting differently in different situations. Certainly, some details of the story have been altered in transmission, but that is not the same as alleging that the story as a whole was not based on an actual event.

It is improbable that such an extraordinary story about a sick man being lowered from the roof of a house should have been recounted unless it had actually taken place. As Meier (1991: vol. 2, p. 680) has written: 'I am inclined to think that some event stuck in the public ministry because of its strange circumstances'. Crossan's proposal (1991: p. 323) that the story is derived from the same event which underlies John 5.1–7 (the healing at the Pool of Bethesda) seems very improbable.

We may conclude that in all likelihood Jesus did heal a man on a pallet bed who had been lowered through the roof of a house. There are those who believe that the Gospels always contain precise historical accounts of events and sayings, and others who hold that very little of the Gospels give an account of what actually happened. The view taken in this study is that, although there have been alterations in transmission and there is no guarantee that the text of the Gospels (in Greek) always gives an accurate account of Jesus' Aramaic words, it is nevertheless reasonable to assume that the Synoptic Gospels do give a generally accurate record unless there is good reason in a particular case to doubt this.

Mark and Luke both explain (but Matthew omits) the strange circumstances in which the paralysed man is brought to Jesus. We must imagine that Jesus was in a single-storey, flat-roofed house (possibly Peter's house in Capernaum), with a door perhaps opening up into a courtyard. Mark and Luke explain that it was not possible to bring the man to Jesus because of the crowd surrounding him, so he was put on a pallet bed, carried up to the roof by four men and lowered through it down to the ground. It is not easy to imagine how this could have been done with safety, and it was sufficiently unusual for this detail to have been remembered.

When Jesus saw the faith of the men who had done this – for they would not have taken all this trouble unless they strongly believed that Jesus could heal their friend – he turned to the man on the pallet bed and said to him: 'Your sins are forgiven.' At this, scribes who were sitting watching thought to themselves that Jesus was blaspheming, for only God can forgive sins. (If all illness was regarded as caused by sin, the very fact that the man was healed becomes blasphemous, as only God can forgive sins.) Mark, the earliest source, describes them as 'reasoning in their hearts' (i.e. not making a verbal protest). This is not picked up by the two subsidiary accounts: Matthew has 'they said within themselves', while Luke reads 'the scribes and the Pharisees began to reason, saying . . .'

However, when it comes to Jesus' response, all three accounts imply that, although the scribes and Pharisees strongly disapproved, they had not actually said anything. Mark reads, 'when Jesus perceived in his spirit that they so reasoned within themselves, he said unto them, "Why reason ye these things in your hearts?"'; Matthew has 'Jesus, knowing their thoughts, said, "Why do you think evil in your hearts?"'; while Luke has 'when Jesus perceived their questionings, he answered them, "Why do you question in your hearts?"' In other words, all three accounts in the Synoptic Gospels go out of their way to point out that Jesus knew without being told what his opponents were thinking.

So there are two sets of sayings which require explanation. First, how did Jesus know without being told that the man was physically paralysed because of a spiritual paralysis caused by guilt? Second, how did Jesus know what his opponents were thinking about the healing?

It has been objected that because Jesus did not believe that illness was the result of sin, he could not have said to the paralytic, 'Your sins are forgiven', but that is to misunderstand the situation. Jesus did not convict the man of sin, but he did try to remove his feelings of guilt. It is well known that feelings of guilt can result in physical disability. How did Jesus suspect that the man had these strong feelings of guilt? Would anyone with normal insight into human nature have been able to detect that? Perhaps, after questioning; but surely not straight away. If so, it would appear that his knowledge was either supernatural or paranormal. Of course there may have been circumstances unknown to us which would explain Jesus' insight. And so a conclusion is only probable.

Moreover, Jesus intuited what his opponents were thinking. Some commentators have suggested that their hostility has been added to the original story (Nineham, 1963: p. 91). But it is not reasonable to reject something just because it is abnormal. Did the scribes and Pharisees show non-verbal signs of their disapproval? Was their disapproval an assumption which Jesus might reasonably have inferred because he knew they did not recognize his Messianic status? According to St Mark's Gospel, this is the first indication of opposition. So there are two possible explanations of Jesus' knowledge of what they were thinking, namely, that he had supernatural powers from God or that he was endowed with paranormal powers of intuiting other people's thoughts. This incident does not prove that Jesus knew these things by telepathy, but at the least it suggests that the idea should be further investigated. And even if Jesus' knowledge of his opponents' thoughts without being told is not historical, the story shows that by the time that St Mark's Gospel was written, people believed it to be true.

As Meier (1991: vol. 2, p. 680) has remarked, 'By the end of the first Christian generation the story has gone through many stages of development'. However, Jesus' immediate realization that the man's paralysis was due to his guilt and his intuitive understanding of his opponents' thoughts are integral parts of the story.

The widow's mite (Mark 12.41–44; Luke 21.1–4)

This episode is one of the few found in Mark and Luke but not in Matthew. Luke's version is shorter than Mark's and it seems, from the number of words that they have in common, that he derived it from Mark. The episode in both Gospels took place after Jesus' last entry into Jerusalem, before he was betrayed. It follows on from a mention of those who take the chief seats in the synagogue and who are accused of 'devour[ing] widows' houses'. So it is extremely apposite in this context and may have been placed at this point because of the earlier mention of widows.

It has been suggested that the episode is really a Jewish parable used by Jesus and transformed into a story, because there are a number of Jewish and pagan parallels (Nineham, 1963: p. 334). It is perhaps hardly surprising that others have noted the contrast between small but costly offerings made by the poor and large offerings by those who can easily afford them. It is possible that the incident is not original but developed in Christian tradition out of the situation described in James 2.1–5. Given, however, that none of the alleged parallels is concerned with offerings to the Jewish treasury, nor are there any verbal similarities, there seems no good reason to deny the historicity of the story.

The moral point that Jesus was making concerns the nature of sacrifice: the offering of a poor widow was worth more than that of rich people who put into the Temple treasury's collection boxes large sums out of their overflowing wealth. Although the poor widow offered a mere couple of coins (the Greek word signifies the lowest possible denomination, less than a penny, somewhat akin to the Indian *pice*), that, we are told, was 'all that she had'. What does that phrase mean? It is improbable that Jesus intended to mean 'all that she had on her', for anyone might find themselves with only very small change and there would be little praise for offering that to the treasury collection box if there was plenty more money at home.

Was Jesus exaggerating? He did sometimes use the common Jewish practice of hyperbole in order to drive home his point (e.g. that is easier for a camel to go through the eye of a needle than for a rich man to enter the kingdom of heaven). Did he use it here? We cannot be certain. One must suppose that the widow had the coins with her because she had intended to buy something with them, probably some food; otherwise they would have been kept securely at home. On an impulse she gave to God all the money that she possessed, small as that was. One can presume that she had grown-up children, and that they would see that she did not starve.

On the supposition that the two coins were indeed all that the widow had, how did Jesus know this? There is no hint in the Gospel texts that he had asked her, and no one else would have told him. If he did know without being told, his knowledge was either supernatural or paranormal – a form of telepathy.

First meeting with Peter and the call of Nathanael (John 1.42–47)

There are particular difficulties associated with the historicity of St John's Gospel. On the one hand, his stories often have precise details and are vividly written and the Evangelist or his source seems to have had accurate knowledge about the topography of the Holy Land – especially in his account of the last week in Jerusalem, where his details are in many respects superior to those of the Synoptic Gospels. On the other hand, John's Gospel contains much material which reads more like an inspired meditation on the life and ministry of Jesus than the accurately recorded speech and action of his subject. His own theological understanding of Jesus' ministry, death and resurrection seems often to intrude, and at times it is not easy to determine what is his own comment and what is intended to be attributed to Jesus. It is therefore necessary to look very carefully before pronouncing on the historicity of any words or incidents.

According to the Synoptic Gospels Jesus called Andrew and Peter while he was walking along the shore of the Sea of Galilee when they, being fishermen, were casting their nets in the water. But St John tells us that Jesus first met them at Bethabara beyond Jordan where John was baptizing. This immediately calls into question the relationship between the Fourth Gospel and the Synoptics: was the author of the Fourth Gospel ignorant of the Synoptics or was he correcting them? Did he have another, more reliable, source than that which lies behind the Synoptic account? It is hard to see why he or his source should have concocted this story, especially since the Johannine account of this period is so precise, even giving the days of the week on which the events he records took place.

Leaving aside the vexed question of John's relationship with the Synoptics, let us turn to the Johannine account of the meeting of Jesus with Simon Peter. His brother Andrew told him that he had found the Messiah and he took him to Jesus; he did not even have to tell Jesus his name. Jesus is recorded as saying: 'Thou art Simon the son of Jona: thou shalt be called Cephas, which is by interpretation, A stone.' Of course it is possible that Andrew had already told Jesus his brother's name, but as we shall see elsewhere in St John's Gospel, Jesus is often depicted as having extraordinary knowledge of others. He did not actually call Simon Cephas at this point: he said that that is what he would be called, as indeed happened, according to Matthew 16.18, in the account of the apostle's confession of Jesus as the Christ at Caesarea Philippi.

The episode in St John's Gospel of John the Baptist's attestation of Jesus, which provides the setting for his words to Peter and Nathanael, marks the end of a development in which Jesus' baptism at the hands of John has finally disappeared, leaving only a revelation about his role, according to Crossan (1991: p. 234). In this case, Jesus' words spoken to Peter and Nathanael would not be historical. This, however, is not an inevitable conclusion. On the assumption that John is narrating what actually took place, what are we to make not only of Jesus' extraordinary knowledge about the name by which Simon would be known, but more importantly of Jesus' immediate realization about his character which enabled him to know that he would become the chief of his followers? Could it have come about through ordinary intuition? That seems improbable. Could it be because Jesus had supernatural knowledge about such matters? That is what the author of the Gospel seems to have assumed. But is this probable? In the Synoptic Gospels Jesus never claimed that he acted like God in this way, nor does it seem compatible with the affirmation earlier in the chapter that the Word was made flesh and dwelt among us. If Jesus was truly God incarnate, he could hardly have had supernatural knowledge of this kind, as he would not be truly human – so the christological argument would run. So how can his knowledge be explained, if the Gospel actually represents the words of Jesus? Only, I suggest, by the hypothesis that Jesus was gifted with telepathy, that is to say, with paranormal powers of knowing what other people were thinking, and paranormal insight into their character.

There follows in St John's Gospel the call of Nathanael. Philip told Nathanael that he whom Moses and the prophets had foretold had been found. Despite his scepticism of anyone who came from Nazareth, Nathanael came to see Jesus. As soon as Jesus saw him, he is said to have immediately read his character – 'an Israelite worthy of the name; there is nothing false in him' (1.47). Nathanael was astonished that Jesus knew him. How did he know him? Did he have divine knowledge of everybody, or was he using a God-given gift of paranormal insight into another's character and mind? We shall examine the passage further when we come to consider clairvoyance, in Chapter 5.

Jesus' reserve towards believers through miracles (John 2.23f.)

According to St John's Gospel, Jesus cleansed the Temple not at the end of his public ministry (as in the Synoptic Gospels), but at its beginning, when he left Galilee to go up to Jerusalem for the Passover. He was already carrying out healings, as a result of which John records that many believed in him. He goes on to inform us that Jesus did not trust them on this account, for he wanted a deeper faith than that which depended upon miracles. The Evangelist writes: 'He knew men so well, all of them, that he needed no evidence from others about a man, for he himself could tell what was in a man' – clearly an editorial addition similar to his disciples' later comment in John 16.30: 'We are certain now that you know everything, and do not need to be questioned; because of this we believe that you have come from God.' John evidently believed that Jesus had a supernatural ability to know another's mind. If he was right, might it not have been a paranormal gift rather than a supernatural power?

Paul claimed that the Holy Spirit enables people to see into the hearts of others (1 Corinthians 14.25); the same thought also occurs in the Talmud. Bultmann (1971: p. 102) has pointed out that this ability was regarded in pagan and Christian Hellenism as the characteristic of *theios anthropos*, the divine man. It was ascribed to the Redeemer in the Mandaean liturgy. Bultmann points out that the wonder-worker Apollonius of Tyana could divine human thoughts, as could a priest of Isis and the astrologist Horus. These were not holy men, and this leads me to think that, if Jesus had this ability, it was more likely to be a paranormal gift of God rather than supernatural knowledge directly given him. Jesus, of course, impressed his disciples by his holiness; and there is sometimes, as we shall see later, a strange connection between holiness and the paranormal.

Jesus and the Samaritan woman (John 4.16–18, 29)

According to John, when Jesus was moving from Judaea to Galilee and passing through Samaria, he stopped on the main road at Jacob's well outside a village called in the Gospel Sychar, where he met a Samaritan woman. The story of this encounter is unique to the Fourth Gospel, and embedded in it is some of the most vivid narrative in that Gospel; and yet there was no one else present other than Jesus and the woman. Jesus had sat down wearily by the well while his disciples had gone into the village to buy some food; he surprised the woman, who had come to draw water, by asking her to give him some water to drink. The Fourth Gospel can hardly have recorded the actual words they used, as they were alone, but it would have been a strange tale for the Evangelist or his source to have made up as it were from scratch. According to John, Jesus told the woman to go back to the town and call her husband, but when he said this to her, he knew without being told that she had no husband – that she had had five husbands but the person with whom she was living was not her husband. (There is surely nothing allegorical in her having had five husbands.) The woman went back to the village and is reported to have said: 'Come and see a man who has told me everything I ever did.'

The author of St John's Gospel has clearly left his mark on the story, not least in Jesus' open declaration that he was the Messiah. If, however, Jesus did speak to a Samaritan woman in these circumstances, she is unlikely to have kept what happened to herself: she would surely have told others about the gist of their conversation and her story would have become widely known. The woman, we are told, was amazed at his knowledge about her past. If this was really the case, the same question must be asked here as has been earlier: how did Jesus know, without being told, about the woman's previous history? Was this supernatural knowledge in which Jesus showed himself to be *theios anthropos*, the God-man, as Bultmann (1971: p. 180) suggests? Or is it another instance of the paranormal gift of knowing what is in another's mind?

The theological value of the story is that Jesus showed himself as giving living water welling up into eternal life and led people to worship the Father in spirit and in truth, for 'God is spirit, and those who worship him must worship in spirit and in truth'.

But Jesus did not have to have knowledge of a person's past life in order to be the Redeemer. And so the question returns: if the story is historically based, is this another instance of his paranormal knowledge?

Jesus' knowledge of the death of Lazarus (John 11.11–14)

The raising of Lazarus is a key landmark in St John's Gospel: it is the last in the series of signs leading to the supreme sign of Jesus' own death and resurrection. According to John, it is this miracle, rather than the cleansing of the Temple, which led the Jewish authorities to decide that Jesus must be put to death, and after this Jesus went into hiding in a small village near the wilderness, emerging only for his last and final visit to Jerusalem. There are those who believe that the Lazarus episode has been placed here to prepare for the story of Jesus' death and resurrection; some regard the whole story as fictitious, possibly derived from the parable of Dives and Lazarus (Luke 16.20ff.) – although if a connection exists between them, it would seem more probable that it is the other way round (Dodd, 1963: p. 230). They find it impossible to find a place for the story in the Marcan outline, although in the Secret Gospel of Mark (an excerpt of which has been found in a letter of Clement of Alexandria) a version of the story which seems in many respects earlier than the Fourth Gospel account, omitting the three days in the tomb, is placed between Mark 10.34 and 35 (Smith, 1973: p. 164). Many find it impossible to believe that someone could be resuscitated after three days in a tomb in a Middle Eastern climate when the body would have already begun seriously to deteriorate.

I am particularly attracted by the suggestion of J. A. T. Robinson (1985: pp. 225f.) that when the Sanhedrin met after the chief priests had been told about the raising of Lazarus (John

11.47–55), they issued a proscription which in the absence of the offender pronounced him guilty unless proved otherwise and thus rendered him liable to death. In Jewish law the prisoner would then have to be interrogated, just as Jesus was later at his trial. Meanwhile he went into hiding in Ephraim, a village bordering on the desert. According to the Talmud Jesus was accused of practising sorcery and leading Israel into apostasy, and for forty days before his death a herald went round asking for evidence in his favour (b. San. 43a) . This seems to refer to the period when Jesus was in hiding before he returned to Jerusalem. If this explanation of the passage in John 11.47–55 holds good, something very strange must have taken place at Bethany over Lazarus which provoked the Jewish authorities into action. Furthermore, if Lazarus is identified with the 'beloved disciple' – and there is good reason why he could be (Sanders, 1968: pp. 29ff.) – the revivification of Lazarus would explain why there was a belief that the beloved disciple would never die. All this tends to vindicate the rough outline of John's account, but not of course the details of the narrative.

John tells us that Jesus was not in Judaea (presumably he was in Galilee) when Lazarus fell ill, but his sisters sent him a message. There is then put into Jesus' mouth words which, from their vocabulary, sound as if they have been written by the Evangelist: 'This sickness is not unto death, but for the glory of God, that the Son of God might be glorified thereby.' Then we are told that Jesus made no move to go to Bethany for two days, and then decided to return, despite remonstrances about his safety by his disciples. After speaking some words which betray Johannine style and phraseology, he said plainly: 'Lazarus is dead.' After that he went back to Judaea and to Bethany, despite Thomas' fear that the journey would end in the death of all of them.

Now did Jesus know that Lazarus had died or is this an editorial insertion into the source which the Evangelist used? It reads as an integral part of the story as it now stands, for Martha all but rebuked him for not having come sooner. According to John, Jesus deliberately delayed two days and said that he was glad for the sake of the disciples that he was not there, on the grounds of their faith. It seems extraordinary to do nothing to prevent Lazarus from dying and then, when he knew that he was dead, to make his way to Bethany to raise him from the dead. The story throughout has traces of Johannine language and theology. The account in Clement of Alexandria's excerpt of the Secret Gospel of Mark, as edited by Fuller, which has nothing about three days in a tomb, but which does tell of Jesus taking Lazarus by the hand and raising him to life, sounds a more authentic account of something that actually happened (Smith, 1973; Fuller, 1975: pp. 7f.). Since Jesus' apparent knowledge that Lazarus had died is an integral part of the story in St John's Gospel, and the passage is liberally peppered with Johannine theology, it would be unsafe to regard this as an account of what actually happened. It does show, however, that the author of St John's Gospel believed that Jesus had unusual – in his view supernatural – powers of knowing that Lazarus had died.

Jesus' knowledge of his betrayer (Mark 14.18–20; Matthew 26.21–3; Luke 22.21–3; John 6.64–71, 13.21–7)

There are those who believe that the only genuine historical fact behind the Gospel accounts of Jesus' death and passion is that he was crucified under Pontius Pilate. For example, Crossan (1991: p. 391) holds that the passion narratives consist of the historicization of prophesies from the Old Testament believed to have been fulfilled in Jesus, and that nothing was known about the historical circumstances because all the disciples deserted him and fled. However, there is in my judgement no need to adopt such a radical stance, if only because the passion narratives could not have developed as they are in the Gospels in such a short time. All four Gospels, in their account of the Last Supper of Jesus with his disciples, record Jesus as knowing who would betray him. This could be portrayed as a vague prediction of the future but, since he spoke of someone present 'who has dipped his hand in the dish' (Mark and Matthew) and to whom he gives a sop (John), and whose 'hand . . . is with me on the table', (Luke) it is clear that Jesus, according to all the accounts, knew at the Last Supper who that person was. While Matthew follows Mark closely, the other Gospels recount the incident somewhat differently, probably drawing their material from different sources. But they all agree that Jesus at the supper knew who would be his betrayer. It is reasonable to assume, in the face of this united testimony from different sources, that Jesus did say that he knew who would betray him.

In the Fourth Gospel, Jesus knew early in his ministry the identity of his betrayer. After Jesus had been speaking in the synagogue in Capernaum, claiming that he was the bread that came down from heaven, he realized without being told that his disciples were 'murmuring' at such teaching. Again we may ask, how did he know this? The Fourth Evangelist notes that 'Jesus knew all along who were without faith and who was to betray him' (6.64). This was a critical time in his public ministry, when many of his disciples left him. There follows a passage which in Johannine language presents a parallel to the Synoptic account of the apostles' confession of faith at Caesarea Philippi. There Peter says: 'You are the Christ' (Mark 8.29); in the Fourth Gospel he says: 'Your words are words of eternal life. We have faith, and we know that you are the Holy One of God' (John 6.69), to which Jesus replies, 'Have I not chosen you, all twelve? Yet one of you is a devil' (John 6.70). The traitor is therefore pinpointed to one of the Twelve.

Had Jesus formed the impression early on that Judas was disaffected as a result of living in close companionship with him? Did he know that Judas was interested in money, since he acted as treasurer for the fellowship? Did he think of Judas as an overeager apocalyptic disciple who wanted to ensure that Jesus died a martyr's death? We do not know the answer to any of these questions, except to note that it is one thing to have suspicions about the loyalty of a companion and quite another to predict that he would be a betrayer. Did Jesus have supernatural knowledge about all things, and therefore about his betrayer, or did he have intuitional knowledge of a telepathic kind which gave him insight into the mind of Judas Iscariot?

These questions must be applied to all seven instances I have given, both from the Synoptic Gospels and from the Fourth Gospel, of Jesus' ability to know what people are thinking and what is happening elsewhere. Admittedly, most of the instances come from the Fourth Gospel, whose author believed that Jesus, as a kind of *theios anthropos*, knew all things. If all of them came from this source, we might well believe that they are a result of the Evangelist's bias. But they do not: we find this knowledge on the part of Jesus about other people in the Synoptic Gospels too. It is perfectly possible to believe that his knowledge was supernatural. But it is equally possible to suppose that it was paranormal telepathy. I do not think that a judgement can be reached until examination has been made of other matters in which Jesus may have had paranormal powers.

Chapter 5

Jesus Sees into the Heart: Clairvoyance

Clairvoyance means literally 'clear seeing', and it is a word used to express the alleged power of perceiving physical, as distinct from mental, events in paranormal fashion. There is some similarity between telepathic and clairvoyant messages, but whereas telepathy is used for the perception of ideas, concepts or even speech, clairvoyance involves communication by means of a visual image, or simply 'seeing' what is happening elsewhere. It seems that there is a stimulation of the visual rather than auditory area of the human cortex, although the means by which this happens is completely unknown. Like telepathy, there are many authenticated instances recorded in *Phantasms of the Living* (Gurney et al., 1918), together with Rhine's card-guessing experiments at Duke University forming a database of over 10,000 cases. Sheldrake (2003: p. 52) has reviewed the history of more recent research, both the transmission of images following on from Rhine's card-guessing experiments, with increasingly rigorous use of *ganzfeld*, and also what is known as 'remote viewing' in which a person 'sees' something happening at some distance. Here is an interesting example of the latter, in an account of a British local government officer in Kenya:

As my boy placed the coffee on my table, he remarked: 'Did you see that the Bwana Katchiku is dead?' 'Where did you get that from?' I asked. 'Chief N'degwa just seen it,' he answered simply. 'Send N'degwa to me,' I told him. N'degwa came immediately . . . He wore the usual kaross made of hyrax skins, and he stood before me and made his customary salute. I took his head and welcomed him. 'What is this?' I asked. 'Bwana Katchiku is dead, do you say? How did you learn this?' 'I see it,' was his astonishing reply. 'When?' I demanded. 'Now,' he said. Somehow I knew he was speaking the truth, nor was there any reason for him to do otherwise . . . Seven days later a runner arrived at my camp with the news that Bwana Katchiku had died, at a distance 250 miles from my camp. I recorded the incident and calculated that he must have passed away a few minutes before I got the message from N'degwa. (Sheldrake, 2003: p. 215)

It is interesting to note that the American CIA was sufficiently impressed to use 'remote viewing' during the Cold War to spy on what was confirmed three years later to be a secret nuclear weapons factory in Kazakhstan.

There is of course no spying in the Gospels, but there are a few passages where 'remote viewing' seems to have taken place.

Nathanael and the fig tree (John 1.48ff.)

We have already noticed a possible case of telepathy with reference to Nathanael, when Jesus immediately recognized his character as guileless. When Nathanael asked Jesus how he knew him, Jesus replied that he had observed him before Philip had approached him with the invitation to come and see him. Jesus is reported to have said, 'Before Philip called you, when you were under the fig tree, I saw you' (1.48). This response astonished Nathanael, and enabled him to acknowledge Jesus as Israel's Messiah, although Jesus seemed to rebuke him for resting his faith on signs and wonders, and told him that he would see 'greater things than these'.

Nathanael in the story clearly recognized the particular occasion when Jesus had 'seen' him, despite the fact that Jesus had not been there. The text of the Gospel does not tell us that Jesus saw Nathanael under *a* fig tree, but under *the* fig tree, the particular place where Nathanael had been before Philip approached him, and where Nathanael remembered he had been. If Jesus had not been there, how could he have seen him there? If the story is true, it is hard to think of any solution to the question other than clairvoyance. Although the point is missed by most writers on the Gospel, one commentator has noted it, recognizing that it was 'due to his [Jesus'] supra-normal faculty of perception' (Sanders, 1968: p. 103).

But is the story true? Apart from the mention of him in the account of John 21.2, Nathanael of Cana is unknown to history. Did he really exist or is the story the result of the Evangelist's fertile imagination? The problems of regarding the account as historical have already been discussed in the chapter on telepathy. The fact that Nathanael's name does not occur in the earliest records outside the Gospel does not necessarily mean that he did not exist; there were others of Jesus' close disciples who were not members of the Twelve. The detail of the fig tree tells in its favour. Even if the words used in *oratio recta* do not represent the exact speech of Jesus and of Nathanael in this encounter, the story may well be based on historical fact. Even if this is denied, it is certainly true that the author of St John's Gospel believed that Jesus was clairvoyant.

The miraculous catch of fish (Luke 5.1–11)

In the Gospels of St Mark and St Matthew, after his temptation Jesus came to Galilee and began his preaching of the kingdom of

God there. Passing by the shore of Lake Galilee he saw Simon and his brother Andrew fishing. He called them to follow him to become fishers of men and they followed him straight away. Similarly, he saw James and John, the two sons of Zebedee, mending their nets with their father. He told them to stop catching fish but to catch men and they too left all and followed him (Mark 1.16–20; Matthew 4.18–22). It is hard to believe that this call to discipleship came out of the blue. Jesus had already begun his preaching of the kingdom of God in Galilee, where he had his headquarters at Capernaum, and the two sets of brothers must have known him and heard him, although we are not told anything about this earlier relationship.

St Luke begins the Galilean ministry of Jesus somewhat differently. According to his Gospel, it opened with a sermon in his home town synagogue at Nazareth, where he was rejected. He went to Capernaum, where he healed a sick man in the synagogue. It was only then that Simon was introduced: Jesus entered Simon's house and healed his sick mother-in-law. From there Jesus went preaching in the local synagogues. At one point he was being pressed by a crowd on the shore of the lake as he addressed them, when he saw two ships nearby with fishermen washing their nets; he got into one of them, which belonged to Simon, and asked him to move a little way out from the shore, so that all the people could hear him. (I have myself waded out from the shore at the traditional spot where this is supposed to have happened, and I can bear witness that from there one can be heard with ease from a long stretch of the shore of the lake.)

St Luke later in the story identified those in the other boat as John and James, the sons of Zebedee, who were in partnership with Simon. When Jesus had finished speaking to the crowds he told Simon to launch out into deeper water and to let down the nets. Although they had been fishing all night and had caught nothing, at Jesus' request they did so, and caught a huge amount of fish – so many that they needed the help of the other boat, and both began to sink. The two sets of brothers were all astonished, while Simon was so moved that he knelt down and said to Jesus: 'Depart from me, for I am a sinful man.' It was then, according to Luke, that they were told that from henceforth they would catch not fish but men, and when they got to the shore, they left everything and followed Jesus.

This Lucan account is very similar to a story of the risen Jesus which is found in the appendix of St John's Gospel (John 21.1–11). The Twelve had returned to Galilee when they left Jerusalem after the resurrection of Jesus, and they decided to go fishing. Again they fished all night and caught nothing. When they came to the shore the next morning they saw a figure whom (hardly surprisingly) they did not immediately recognize as the risen Jesus. He asked them if they had caught anything. When they said 'No', he told them to cast their net on the right side of the boat and they could not draw it aboard because of the huge catch of fish. The disciple whom Jesus loved, whoever he may have been, was the first to recognize Jesus, and when he told Simon, Simon jumped in and swam to Jesus. The others brought the ship to shore, dragging the net: there were 153 fish but the net was not broken. When they got to the shore they found a fire, and were given bread and told to eat some of the fish that they had caught.

What is the relationship between the two stories?. There seem to be added details of a symbolic kind in the Johannine story; the unbroken net, the 153 fish representing the nations of the world (how would such a large number of fish have been actually counted?), and the Eucharistic undertones of the breakfast by the shore. On the other hand, it has been suggested that Simon's remark, 'Depart from me, for I am a sinful man', would be more appropriate in a resurrection story after he had three times denied Jesus when he was arrested (Creed, 1942: p. 73). But it can equally be explained as a suitable response to the feeling of transcendence induced by Jesus' words. (The mention of a charcoal fire on both occasions [Crossan, 1991: p. 410] is probably not particularly significant since such fires were commonplace.) Again, the promise to make the disciples 'fishers of men' is not necessarily to be seen as a post-resurrection promise since Jesus in his earthly life sent the apostles out on a preaching mission.

Luke inserts the episode into the Marcan account after Mark 1.39. This need not imply that it is secondary material: the Evangelists were not writing biographical history and felt quite free to alter the order in which a pericope was placed. It has been suggested that Luke borrowed the idea of Jesus telling parables to the crowds from a boat from Mark 4.1ff. This is found in Matthew 13.1 but is absent from the Lucan equivalent in Luke 8.4. We may surely assume, however, that Jesus used a boat on more than one occasion to speak to crowds on the shore, and that Luke saw no reason to repeat this. It has also been commented that there is an awkwardness in the way in which John and James, the sons of Zebedee, are introduced near the end of the Lucan account (but Luke surely had to do this if he was not following Mark's account of their call by the seashore) and also in the way in which Jesus asked them to move out into deeper water if he had earlier asked them to come closer in to the shore (though this is no real objection if he knew where the fish were to be found).

On the whole, it is best to regard the Lucan account as historically based and to regard the Johannine version as dependent upon St Luke or on his source, since elsewhere John can alter the Synoptic course of events to fit in with his theological plan (e.g. in moving the cleansing of the Temple to the beginning of the public ministry) and, as already noted, there are signs of Johannine additions that can be seen in his narrative, not least in Eucharistic overtones in the meal which Jesus shares with his disciples on the seashore and evangelistic resonances of the 153 fish caught.

Crossan (1991: p. 410) suggests that the religious meaning of the story is that to fish all night without the risen Jesus is to catch nothing. But why only after the resurrection? Caird (1971: p. 91) has pointed out 'Jesus's influence with dispirited men, wearied by a night of profitless toil. These were the men he needed for his disciples, disciplined by labour and hardship, but with the impetuous loyalty to say, "If you give the order, I will do it."'

The question remains: is the narrative based on what actually happened? As I have pointed out, it is improbable that the story was a Lucan creation, made up from the saying that Jesus would make his disciples fishers of men. The story hardly seems to illustrate that saying. It is more probable that Jesus, having made use of their boat for preaching to the crowds, wanted an appropriate way of saying thank you, and did this by pointing out where a shoal of fish was swimming. Yet he was no fisherman; he had followed Joseph's trade as a builder or worker in wood, and it appears from Eusebius (*Ecclesiastical History*, 3.20) that his family – or at least his brother's family – were simple agricultural labourers. The two sets of brothers were fishermen and they would have been far more likely to know where a shoal of fish was situated than Jesus. Nor is it credible to suppose that the shoal was invisible to them because of diffraction in the water, whereas it would have been visible to Jesus. Either Jesus had supernatural knowledge of where the fish were or he had the paranormal gift of 'remote viewing'. Surely, if he had supernatural knowledge, he would not have used it for such an apparently trivial purpose?

Knowledge of healing carried out at a distance (Matthew 8.5–13; Luke 7.1–10; John 4.47–54)

There are considerable divergences between the three accounts here. According to John, the person healed was the son of a nobleman and presumably Jewish; according to the Synoptics, he was the servant of a centurion, and so a Gentile. However, the Greek *pais* can designate either a son or a servant. In Matthew the sick servant is paralysed; in John he is at the point of death. The Gentile centurion is praised for his faith, the like of which Jesus said he had not seen in all Israel, while the (Jewish) noble-man is rebuked with the words: 'Unless you see signs and wonders you will not believe.' In Q too there are differences between the two versions of Matthew and Luke. According to Matthew, the centurion speaks directly to Jesus, while in Luke his appeal for help comes through intermediaries. In view of the sayings added to the Lucan account, it would seem that Matthew's version is closer to the Q original. Evidently there has been considerable development in all the accounts. At the same time the tale may well have a historical foundation, as Meier points out (1991: vol. 2, p. 726): both John and the Synoptics place the story in Capernaum; there is multiple attestation; there are semitisms in the Q accounts; there is discontinuity and embarrassment at the faith of a Gentile.

According to John, Jesus said to the nobleman, 'Your son lives', while in Matthew he is reported to have said, 'Because of your faith, so let it be.' Luke recounts that it was the centurion's servants who told him that his servant was alive. We have already concluded that the Matthean account is more likely to be nearer to the event than Luke's, while the Johannine account, with its reference to 'signs and wonders', bears traces of Johan-nine theology. It follows that Matthew's assertion that Jesus knew that the servant had been healed is part of the original story. In which case, how did Jesus know? Was his knowledge supernatural? There is no suggestion in the Gospels that this was the case. Or did he have the gift of clairvoyance?

Chapter 6

Jesus' Foresight: Precognition

Precognition, as the derivation of the word implies, means knowing about something before it has happened; it is used when such knowledge has not come from any known source. In every age there have been those who have claimed to know the future, whether by oracular utterances as at Delphi, or in later ages by the words of fortune-tellers. The phenomenon has often been explained as a result of inference from known facts or intentions, intelligent guesswork or even the sheer coincidence of something happening in the same way in which it has been foretold.

Precognition may happen in human beings and in nature (e.g. when animals have extraordinary knowledge of a coming earthquake). It has been the subject of psychical research and has been studied experimentally. J. B. Rhine found that in card-guessing a person might guess, not the card that had been turned up, but the next card that had not yet been shown. Precognition happens from time to time spontaneously: take this example of an American officer during the Second World War who was driving along an autobahn during the invasion of Germany:

All of a sudden I got the still small voice. Something was wrong with the road, I just knew it. I stopped, amid the groans and jeers of the other two. I started walking along the road. About fifty yards from where I had left the jeep I found out what was wrong. We were about to go over a bridge – only the bridge wasn't there. It had been blown up and there was a sheer drop of about 75 feet. (Sheldrake, 2003: p. 234)

There are many certified instances of precognition having occurred (Tyrrell, 1947: pp. 73ff.) and collections of well-attested stories (Hearne, 1989). Although according to Louise Rhine's database 60 per cent of instances occurred in dreams, they also occurred when people were wide awake. Many related to bad news. One of the more moving stories is the account of a small girl in the Welsh village of Aberfan who began talking of dying and who said she would be with her best friends Peter and June. She also dreamt of going to school and there was no school there because something black had come all over it. She went to school and was killed in a landslide which engulfed the site, and she was buried beside Peter and June (Enright, 1995: p. 339).

One might expect to find instances of precognitions in the accounts of the Jewish prophets in the Bible, since one of the meanings of prophecy is prediction. But in fact the canonical prophets were primarily God's representatives, his messengers, his servants. Occasionally, however, we do find them making predictions. Jeremiah (29.10) prophesied an exile for seventy years (a round number: actually it was sixty-one years) and Isaiah foretold Israel's return from exile. But generally they spoke the word of God to their generation in spiritual and moral terms.

There are some instances of apparent precognition in the Gospels which deserve to be investigated.

The threefold prediction of the Passion (Mark 8.27ff.; 9.30f.; 10.32ff.; Matthew 16.21ff.; 17.22ff.; 20.17ff. and Luke 9.22ff.; 9.44f.; 18.31ff.

On three occasions during Jesus' public ministry, in all three Synoptic Gospels, there is a solemn warning by him to his disciples of his coming death and resurrection. It has been said that these sound like the solemn notes of a funeral bell presaging his coming demise.

The first occasion follows Peter's confession of faith in Jesus as Messiah, about which the disciples are warned not to tell anyone. Jesus' prediction of his coming death caused Peter to rebuke him because Jesus said that the Messiah would have to suffer. In turn, Jesus rebuked Peter in stinging terms for his worldly attitude. The story is similar in all three Gospels, with Matthew adding after Peter's confession Jesus' commendation of Peter, and with Luke omitting Peter's rebuke to Jesus and Jesus' stinging reply. The warning about what is to come is quite explicit, 'that the Son of man must suffer many things, and be rejected by the elders and the chief priests and the scribes, and be killed, and after three days rise again'.

The second prediction occurs in all three Gospels as the disciples made their way incognito through Galilee to Jerusalem. Here the prophecy is not so explicit: Jesus 'was teaching his disciples, saying to them, "The Son of man will be delivered into the hands of men, and they will kill him; and when he is killed, after three days he will rise."' Mark adds that the disciples did not understand the saying, but they were too frightened to ask for clarification. Matthew follows Mark, but Luke omits mention of their lack of understanding and as a substitute he records that the saying made them very sad.

The third prediction also occurs in all three Synoptic Gospels while they were on the way to Jerusalem. It is much more explicit even than the first prediction: 'the Son of man will be delivered up to the chief priests and the scribes, and they will condemn him to death, and deliver him to the Gentiles; and they will mock him, and spit upon him, and scourge him, and kill him; and after three days he will rise.' The wording is pretty much the same in all three Gospels, and Luke adds here what he omitted about the second prediction – that the disciples did not understand what was being said.

These predictions have rightly caused some perplexity among commentators. Were these warnings really given? If Jesus knew he had to suffer, why was he bothered because one of his number would betray him and thus cause him to suffer? Why did not the disciples heed what Jesus was telling them? If Jesus warned them three times, how could they not have known what he meant? Is the comment that their minds were blinded a genuine one or was it added to give some sort of explanation for their coming ignorance of what was to happen to Jesus? For they ran away when he was arrested, and they were dumbfounded at the resurrection appearances. There is no easy explanation of these difficulties, other than the supposition that all three predictions are fabrications. Why fabricate them, though, if the disciples took no notice of them? It does not seem reasonable to assume that they could have been made up to put the disciples in a bad light or to show that what was to happen to Jesus was inexorable divine destiny. But if they have a historical basis, were there really *three* solemn sayings? Could the disciples really not have understood after *three* warnings? Perhaps Jesus spoke only in general terms. Perhaps there were only one or two predictions of what was to come, and that in guarded language. There is no certain solution to this problem, but it makes much more sense to recognize that at least one of the predictions is historically grounded, even though with the benefit of hindsight we may conclude that the accounts probably now include more details than Jesus himself actually gave.

Granted that the predictions have a historical foundation, would they have been a reasonable inference for Jesus to make having already met with opposition in the past which might be expected to increase when he went back to Jerusalem? It did not inevitably follow from this that he would have to die. And what about his resurrection? In Mark 10.45 he said that the Son of Man came to give his life as a ransom for many (surely an authentic phrase), but there is no hint that this ransom would be followed by resurrection, and in the passion stories there is also no hint of a belief that he would be raised from the dead. When in the Garden of Gethsemane he prayed that this cup would be taken from him, he was surely not thinking of resurrection after death. Perhaps the original prediction mentioned only death and not resurrection, with the latter being added later with the benefit of hindsight.

We may conclude that, if Jesus had a fully human nature, we need not suppose that he would have necessarily inferred from what had happened to him in the past what was going to happen to him in the future. So we are back at the same kind of question that has been asked before in this study. Did Jesus have supernatural knowledge of the future, or did he have paranormal insight into what was going to happen? To decide this question, let us look at other instances of Jesus' predictions.

The donkey on which Jesus rode into Jerusalem (Mark 11.1–11; Matthew 21.1–9; Luke 19.28–38)

The story about Jesus' disciples fetching the animal on which he would ride into Jerusalem is substantially the same in all three Synoptic Gospels, except that Matthew mentions both an ass and a colt, apparently so as to show the fulfilment of Zechariah 9.9, which he quotes in his version. It is obviously an enlargement of St Mark's account, for Jesus could not have ridden on both

animals. As Borg (1997: p. 136) has written: 'Matthew's alter-
ation of Mark's story illustrates the difference between "history
remembered" and "prophecy historicised" and its meaning.'

The religious meaning of the episode is clear: Jesus did not
want to ride into the Holy City on a horse, an emblem of power,
but humbly on a lowly donkey. The Messiah was expected to
come to Jerusalem via the Mount of Olives; but it is not clear
whether Jesus intended his entry to be that of a Messiah coming
to his city, or whether he simply intended a humble entry. If not
Messianic, in fulfilment of Zechariah, the entry on a donkey was
certainly symbolic. If the latter, it may well have been his way of
carrying out the 'Messianic secret', comparable to his earlier
instructions to his disciples to tell no one that he was the Christ.
However, as pilgrims were expected to enter Jerusalem on foot,
it is hard to see how a Messianic meaning could have been
avoided. Jesus and his disciples were greeted by an enthusiastic
crowd, probably small enough not to provoke opposition from
the authorities. Bultmann (1931: p. 281) calls the story a 'Messianic legend', and Dibelius (1934: p. 122) a 'cultus legend', but
both agree that it may be based on fact. It is reasonable to assume
that Jesus did enter the city on a donkey.

But how did he obtain it? The party had walked from Jericho,
surely a tiring journey from the Rift Valley over the wilderness
to the capital city. Mark says they came to Bethphage and
Bethany before descending by the Mount of Olives, but actually
they would have passed them in the reverse order, Bethphage
being closer to Jerusalem. When they got there, Jesus told two
disciples to go to the village opposite (it is not named) and there
they would find a colt on which no one had ever ridden. They
were to loose it and bring it to Jesus. If anyone asked them what
they were doing, they were to say: 'The Lord has need of it
and will send it back here immediately.' They went and found
the colt tethered at a door in the street; the bystanders did

indeed ask them what they were doing, to which they answered as Jesus had told them; and they brought the colt to Jesus.

Is the story genuine? It is probable that the phrase 'on which no one had ever ridden' has been added so as to make the entry accord with Zechariah's prophecy. In most villages in those days it was quite likely that a colt would be tethered in the street. The words 'The Lord has need of it' were probably not the actual words used: perhaps it was some such phrase as 'Our Master needs it and will return it directly'. Perhaps these are the 'legendary elements' to which one commentator refers, who goes on to ask whether the ass's colt actually played the part assigned to it (Nineham, 1963: p. 293). Another commentator writes of the colt being there 'by previous arrangement' (Taylor, 1952: p. 452). Another writes: 'It is probable that the ass was borrowed from a village where our Lord already had friends, and that the owner readily lent it for the use of the Master. The suggestion of an apparently miraculous prevision on the part of our Lord is probably to be set down simply to the point of view from which the story is told by the Evangelist' (Rawlinson, 1944: p. 152).

Are we to assume that Mark made up the story (adding the names of actual villages) because he wanted to show Jesus entering the Holy City in accordance with Zechariah's prophecy, realizing (as Matthew didn't) that the mention of the foal of an ass in addition to an ass did not imply that there were two beasts, but merely conformed to Jewish literary parallelism? It is easier to assume that the story is based on what actually happened. It is difficult to see how a previous arrangement had been made with the owner of the colt if the party had only just arrived from Jericho: are we really to suppose that Jesus, while still in Jericho, sent a message somehow or other to his friends in the village concerned to ask for the loan of the colt on which to ride into Jerusalem? That assumption is more difficult than the acceptance of the story as it stands. If Jesus knew there would be a colt there (presumably there was none in Bethphage, the village at which he had just arrived), it needs to be asked how he knew it was there. Here again we are faced with a choice: was it a natural assumption, did he have supernatural knowledge, or did he have the paranormal faculty of precognition?

Jesus' prophecy of the fall of the Temple (Mark 13.1–4; Matthew 24.1–3; Luke 21.5–7; John 2.19–21)

It is widely recognized that the apocalyptic discourses in the Synoptic Gospels do not contain the actual words spoken by Jesus, and have been affected by later events. For example, the Marcan apocalypse, followed by Matthew, has a reference to the 'abomination of desolation standing where it ought not', which may well be a general reference to an event that occurred way back in 168 BC (1 Maccabees 1.54); but more probably it refers to the attempt by Caligula to have his statue placed in the Temple, an occurrence fortunately prevented by his assassination in AD 41 (Josephus, *Antiquities* xviii.8). Luke, on the other hand, refers as his key point to the time 'when you see Jerusalem surrounded by armies', presumably a reference to the capture of the city in AD 70.

However, there is good evidence that Jesus did on occasion speak in apocalyptic terms (if not in the actual words in the Gospels), as when he is reported to have said, 'I beheld Satan as lightning fall from heaven' (Luke 10.18). Moreover, there is no good reason to doubt the substantial accuracy of the introduction to the apocalyptic discourses found in all three Gospels, which comprises Jesus' prophecy of the fall of the Jewish Temple that took place in AD 70. It was a matter of which we are told he was accused at his trial although the witnesses could not agree about what he had actually said (Mark 14.58; Matthew 26.60). It was a matter about which he is reported to have been mocked while crucified on his cross (Mark 15.29f.), where Jesus is taunted with having said he would rebuild it in three days.

The reference to rebuilding the Temple in three days is found also in the Fourth Gospel (John 2.19). It is placed immediately after the Johannine account of Jesus' 'cleansing' of the Temple, which comes near the beginning of the Gospel rather than during Jesus' last week in Jerusalem. (I find it hard to agree with Crossan's view that the Temple cleansing was a 'symbolic' destruction [Crossan, 1991: p. 357]). Jesus is reported to have said: 'Destroy this temple, and in three days I will raise it up' (John 2.19). This carries the Johannine comment that Jesus was speaking of the temple of his body; but nowhere else did Jesus speak of his body in such terms. Nevertheless it may well have been that Jesus did say something about three days, because John goes out of his way to inform us that after the resurrection the disciples remembered that he had said this, and realized to what he was referring.

Whatever the origin of the reference to three days, it is probable that Jesus did prophesy the coming destruction of the Temple, even though witnesses at his trial could not agree about his actual words (Mark 14.58). It seems unlikely that this prophecy developed after the fall of the Temple, because his reported words in Mark 13 – 'Do you see these great buildings? There will not be left here one stone upon another, that will not be thrown down' – are not strictly accurate, as the present-day existence of the Wailing Wall with its Temple stones bears witness. It is difficult to imagine a prophecy of Jesus being made up which did not come entirely true.

The outbreak of the Jewish war against Rome did not begin until the late 60s. Jesus' death took place over thirty years before, in the early 30s. Of course the Jews then resented the Roman occupation of their land, and there was occasional trouble, as when Pontius Pilate brought Roman ensigns with their effigies into the Holy City; there was even a massacre when Jews protested against the use of sacred money to increase the city's water supply (Josephus, *Antiquities* xviii.3). But at that stage no one could have foretold from present events their eventual outcome in a terrible war over a quarter of a century later. So how was it that Jesus knew about the future destruction of the Jewish Temple? How was he in a position to make this terrible prophecy? Was it because he was given supernatural knowledge or did he have paranormal powers of foresight?

Preparations for the Passover (Mark 14.12–16; Matthew 26.17–19; Luke 22.7–13)

All three Synoptic Gospels give a very similar account of the preparations for the Passover meal which was Jesus' last supper with his disciples, with Matthew shortening the account of how the two disciples whom Jesus sent to do this found their way to the appointed place. According to Mark and Luke, the disciples asked Jesus on Passover morning where they would eat the Passover meal in the evening. Jesus told two of them to go into the city, where a man would meet them carrying a jar of water. They were to follow him to where he was going, where they were to say to the houseowner that the Teacher wanted them to be shown the upper room where they were to eat the Passover; and they would be shown it. The two disciples carried out these instructions and found a large room in readiness, and they made preparations for the Passover meal.

Jesus, having been in the city on earlier occasions, would have had friends there, so he could have arranged earlier for the Twelve to eat the Passover in the house of one of his friends, as custom demanded that it must be eaten within the city bounds. There is nothing particularly surprising in that, although the narrative gives no indication of a prior arrangement and Jesus in the account did not take the initiative; he waited until the disciples asked him where they would eat the Passover.

What is odd, however, is the way in which two of his disciples found out where this would be. They were to meet a man carrying a jar of water and to follow him. The story must surely be grounded in a historical event, because it is very difficult to imagine that such enigmatic instructions could be unhistorical. Perhaps Jesus gave more details which are not included in the Gospels. Even so, it is difficult to understand how an arrangement could have been made with Jesus' friends in the city that someone would be waiting somewhere, and the two disciples would follow him. There must have been many people carrying water in the city (although they would generally have been women), and since a person waiting for Jesus' disciples would not have known them, he would not have been able to recognize them. In any case we are not told that he was waiting for them – people don't usually stand about with heavy jars of water! Was this arrangement made to ensure secrecy? Hardly, for Jesus made no secret of his disciples; and in any case he had been openly teaching in the Temple earlier that week (Mark 14.49). How did Jesus know that they would meet the water-bearer, and recognize him, and so find out where they had to go?

There are some similarities between this story and the earlier account of fetching the ass's colt on which Jesus rode into the Holy City. But there are differences too. In the earlier story a definite place is mentioned, while in this story the two disciples did not know where they were going. In the earlier account, the two disciples did not know whether the colt's owner would be there, while in this story they talked with the houseowner. Although there are similarities, there is nothing inherently difficult in regarding them as grounded in somewhat similar events. But is the story authentic? It seems curiously detached from verse 7 which follows, which simply recounts that the Twelve arrived for the Passover. The disciples were usually described as the Twelve, and much more was needed than making ready the room: the special food for the Passover had to be prepared. All this is said to have happened on the 'first day of unleavened bread', which is usually regarded as being the day after the Passover meal, not the same day. It is possible that the story was later attached to the description of the meal, but this does not in itself make the story inauthentic.

Many commentators reject the story as unhistorical, largely because it seems to show evidence of supernatural foresight on the part of Jesus (Wellhausen, 1903), and Bultmann (1931) regards it as a legend. On the other hand, many commentators regard it as authentic tradition. Once again the question arises: if it is historical, does Jesus show authentic supernatural foresight or is this due to his paranormal gift of prediction?

The prophecy of Judas' treachery (Mark 14.18–20; Matthew 26.20–5; Luke 22.21; John 6.70–1; 13.21–30)

All four Gospels depict Jesus as foretelling the coming treachery of Judas Iscariot at the Last Supper. John first mentions this much earlier, after many of his disciples had left him and Peter had just made his confession of faith, to which Jesus replied: 'Have I not chosen you, all twelve? Yet one of you is a devil', upon which the Evangelist comments: 'He meant Judas, son of Simon Iscariot. He it was who would betray him, and he was one of the Twelve.' (Calling Judas a devil brings to mind that the Fourth Evangelist later said that Satan entered into Judas before he left the company to betray Jesus.) Although the betrayer is not named at this point, it is made clear that he would come from the inner group, one of the Twelve.

Mark and Matthew describe how Jesus told the disciples at the beginning of the meal that there was a betrayer among them at the Last Supper: 'Truly I say to you, one of you will betray me.' At this the Twelve were very distressed and asked who it would be, Jesus answering: 'It is one of the twelve, one who is dipping bread into the dish with me.' He goes on to say that it would better for that man never to have been born. Luke has a slightly different context for the prophecy: in his Gospel it takes place after the institution of the Eucharist, with Jesus saying that the hand of the betrayer was with him at the table. John describes the prediction in yet another way: Peter spoke to the 'disciple whom Jesus loved' (whoever he may have been), as a result of which Jesus was asked who is the betrayer; and he replied: 'It is the man to whom I give this piece of bread when I have dipped it in the dish.' Then after dipping it in the dish, he took it out and gave it to Judas, the son of Simon Iscariot.

What is clear from all accounts is their common agreement that Jesus knew that Judas would betray him. There is no point, for our purposes, in trying to discover which Gospel gives the most accurate account of what happened. It seems strange that John should have invented the conversation between Peter and the disciple whom Jesus loved about the betrayer if it did not occur; but it is equally strange that, when Jesus pointed out who was to betray him (by giving the sop to Judas), they apparently did nothing to prevent him. According to the Synoptics, Jesus never actually named Judas as the one who would betray him, so that they might not have known whom to stop. Again, we need not inquire too closely here why Judas did betray him: whether he wanted money (as the Gospels suggest); or whether he wanted Jesus to prove his messiahship openly when he was arrested; or whether he had simply lost faith in Jesus. What does matter for our purposes is that Judas betrayed him and Jesus knew it would be so.

How did he know? Was it a reasonable inference from Judas' earlier behaviour? 'That Jesus should have read the mind of

Judas and prophesied betrayal is intelligible' (Taylor, 1945: p. 539). It may be intelligible but is it probable? The Gospels give us no hint as to what such a belief would have been based upon: Judas kept the company's finances but that does not prove that he betrayed him for money; there is no impression of Judas' loss of faith in Jesus or that he wanted him to prove his Messiahship after his arrest. What grounds had Judas given Jesus for him to know that Judas would betray him? By the total absence of any indication from the Gospels it seems unlikely that there were any.

Surely we can dismiss the possibility that Jesus' prophecy of Judas' betrayal came into being because the early Church wanted to show Jesus as master of his fate. It is far more likely that the prophecy, found in all four Gospels, is historically grounded. Once more, we can say only that it was through his divine and supernatural knowledge, or that it was the result of his paranormal gift of prediction.

Peter's denial (Mark 14.29; Matthew 26.33; Luke 22.32f.)

Peter in the Gospels is clearly the chief of the Twelve. Yet he is the one who denied Jesus three times, and Jesus himself told him it would be so. On the way to Gethsemane after the Last Supper it seemed that the company sang the Hallel, which is part of the Passover supper liturgy. According to Mark, followed by Matthew, Jesus told the Twelve (and any others who were with them) that they would all fall away from their faith in him, whereupon Peter responded: 'Everyone else may fall away, but I will not.' Jesus contradicts him: 'I tell you this: today, this very night, before the cock crows twice, you yourself will disown me three times.' Luke has a similar prophecy but in a somewhat different context, for he records that after the Last Supper, before they went to the Mount of Olives, a dispute had broken out between them about who should be greatest. Jesus intervened, and said to Peter: 'Simon, Simon, take heed: Satan has been given leave to sift all of you like wheat; but for you I have prayed that your faith may not fail; and when you have come to yourself, you must lend strength to your brothers.' It is after that that Luke records the words about Peter's future denial.

All Gospels record the three instances of Peter's denial when Jesus was being questioned in the High Priest's house and Peter was standing outside in the courtyard. St John's Gospel does not include Jesus' prophecy about the denial; it does, however, include Peter's threefold denial at the house of Caiaphas (John 18.24f.) in a rather different account of Jesus' trial at the hands of the Jewish authorities. At the third denial, the three Synoptic Gospels record that a cock crowed twice, and Peter burst into tears.

Whether or not the trial took place in the High Priest's house as recorded in St Mark's Gospel has been much debated. Whatever happened or did not happen in the High Priest's house, it is very unlikely that the story of Peter's threefold denial comes from later tradition, for who could have made up such a tale about the chief of the Apostles, especially as it appears first in Mark, traditionally the Petrine Gospel? How did Jesus know that Peter would deny him? Was it a legitimate inference from his somewhat impetuous character? Hardly so, for Peter was his most vociferous supporter and the leader of the band. Yet again we must pose the question: was Jesus given supernatural knowledge of what would happen or did he exercise a paranormal gift of precognition?

Chapter 7

The Transfiguration: Luminosity

Mark 9.2–8; Matthew 17.1–3; Luke 9.28–36

So far the reader may well be in two minds about the probability that Jesus exercised paranormal gifts. A consideration of the occasions when Jesus may have used telepathy, clairvoyance and precognition may well leave them with an open mind. However, in the passage that is to be considered now, it is very difficult to find a normal explanation. I refer to what is generally known as the transfiguration.

The story appears in all three Synoptic Gospels in substantially the same form. It does not appear in the Fourth Gospel; in a sense it has no need of it since, according to its author, glory is manifest throughout the public ministry of Jesus and especially in his death and resurrection.

The transfiguration, apart from the events of Jesus' passion, is the only dated event in the Gospels; we are told that it took place six days after Peter's confession of faith at Caesarea. Whether this is a historical reminiscence or is modelled on the six days Moses spent in the cloud on Mount Sinai before his converse with God is not really relevant to our inquiry. Luke, however, tells us that it took place not six days but about eight days later. According to the Gospels, Jesus took Peter and James and John up a high mountain on their own, although the mountain is not specified. Jesus was transfigured in their sight – the Greek word used by Mark and Matthew suggests a change of form or shape.

His clothes became dazzling white, 'with a whiteness no bleacher on earth could equal'. Luke alone records that this took place while Jesus was praying (not the only time that Luke, in contrast to the other Synoptics, mentions Jesus at prayer).

Luke alone tells us that Peter and his companions went into a deep sleep, probably tired after a long climb, and then they woke up. All three Gospels tell how they found Jesus talking with Elijah and Moses (whom somehow they recognized). According to Luke, they were talking about Jesus' departure, presumably meaning his death. Then Peter made an apparently nonsensical remark, asking whether he should make three shelters for them (surely not an easy task on a mountain top where there was little vegetation), but we are told that he did not know what he was saying. Some commentators think that the mention of making tents is an allusion to God tabernacling with humankind, but this hardly explains *three* tents. The remark is so perplexing that it is hard to imagine it as a development of the story. Then the account continues with a cloud overshadowing them, out of which came a voice saying: 'This is my beloved Son: hear him.' When the cloud lifted, Jesus was alone with his three companions. When they were coming down from the mountain, Jesus told them not to tell anyone about it until he rose from the dead, a somewhat strange remark, for earlier, when Jesus had predicted his death and resurrection, we are told that they did not take in his words.

Could it be that this is a piece of symbolic writing such as is found in the apocalyptic writings of first-century Judaism and early Christianity? There is no known parallel to the story elsewhere. A good many commentators think of it as a legend or symbolic tale; others regard it as an account of a post-resurrection event which has been placed at this point for theological reasons. For example, Crossan (1991: p. 389) dismisses its present context without comment in a throwaway sentence: 'Jesus's resurrection–ascension accompanied by two

heavenly beings was rewritten as his transfiguration accompanied by Elijah and Moses in Mark 9.2–8.' But none of the
resurrection stories contain any trace of transfiguration: on the
contrary, there seems to have been some difficulty in recognizing the post-resurrection Jesus from other people, so he must
have looked normal. Those who do not place the story in its
present context do this largely because they do not regard Jesus
as an apocalyptic visionary, despite such sayings in the Gospels
as 'I watched how Satan fell, like lightning, out of the sky' (Luke
10.18). Once the apocalyptic nature of some of Jesus' sayings is
accepted, there is no good reason why the vision (as it is called
in Matthew 17.9) should not have taken place during his public
ministry. The fact that the transfiguration of Jesus appears in all
three Gospels with a particular date attached to it (even if the
date is slightly different in St Luke's Gospel) is a strong reason
against regarding it as a post-resurrection event transferred to
the earthly ministry of Jesus. It is misguided to dismiss an
account of a phenomenon in its current context because it is
contrary to normality.

The religious message of this event is clear: the sonship of
Jesus was revealed to him at his baptism by a heavenly voice, and
the same sonship is revealed to the inner circle of the Twelve on
the Mount of Transfiguration. The whiteness of his body and his
clothes manifests his glorified body, 'the sort of body generally
supposed to belong to heavenly beings and indeed to be the
vesture of God himself' (Boobyer, 1942: p. 23). Commentators
are divided whether this was believed to presage the resurrection
of Jesus or his coming in glory, although the latter seems the
more likely. The event is a key point in Jesus' public ministry:
behind him lay the successes of Galilee, ahead of him lies the
prospect of suffering and death. It is noteworthy that according
to Luke, he was speaking to Moses and Elijah of his 'exodus' that
was to come. The figures of Moses and Elijah are important too,

symbolizing the Law and the Prophets, the work of whom is fulfilled in Jesus. No one knew where Moses was buried, and the belief that he was still alive is shown by an apocalyptic work called 'The Assumption of Moses' (cf. Charles, 1913: pp. 407–24), while Elijah was believed to have been taken into heaven in a chariot of fire.

However, we are not primarily concerned here with the meaning of these events, but whether they took place. The appearance of Elijah and Moses seems part of a visionary experience, together with the cloud, which may be regarded as symbolic of the divine presence, like the cloud, that guided the Israelites through their desert wanderings by day. So too we may regard the voice confirming Jesus' sonship as an auditory aspect of this vision, similar to the voice at Jesus' baptism when he had a visionary experience of the heavens opening and a dove resting upon him. On the other hand, all these phenomena could be seen as expansions in tradition of Jesus' transfiguration, which marked him out as fulfilling that for which the prophets and the lawgiver stood for, and which showed him to be visited by the Shekinah, the divine presence, and which convinced the disciples of his divine sonship. But all these are based on the supposition that Jesus was transfigured.

Let us look more closely at Jesus' luminosity. It is important to note that Luke reports that Jesus was at prayer when all this took place. In all three Gospels he was transfigured: he and his clothes appeared in dazzling white. It can hardly be explained as a myth developed to show how Christ was the fulfilment of Moses, whose face was said to have shone when he came down from Mount Sinai (Exodus 34.30). It is difficult to believe that an event which is a key point of Jesus' ministry is merely based on a myth.

Evelyn Underhill (1913: p. 116) pointed about many years ago that intense communion with God can bring a supernatural radiance to the body, and instanced the lives of St Teresa of Avila, St Catherine of Bologna, St Catherine of Genoa and St Francis of Assisi. Ramsey (1949: p. 107) in the light of this has suggested 'that the Transfiguration itself may lie in the region not of a vision of the disciples but in a real occurrence in our Lord's soul and body'. It is not impossible that St Paul was referring to this luminosity in 2 Corinthians 3.18: 'We all reflect as in a mirror the splendour of the Lord; thus we are transfigured into his likeness, from splendour to splendour; such is the influence of the Lord who is Spirit.'

It is here that we touch on the paranormal: the extraordinary whiteness that encompassed Jesus and his clothes is instanced in a far greater number of cases than the few saints mentioned above. A brilliant light was seen on occasion when Philip Neri, Charles Borromeo, Ignatius of Loyola, Francis de Sales and many more were preaching or celebrating, all people of acknowledged holiness. In Fr Thurston's book (Thurston, 1952) on the physical phenomena of mysticism a whole chapter is devoted to this subject. He writes that it is unquestionably true that there are literally hundreds of examples of luminosity in hagiographical records and, although a great number of these rest on insufficient testimony, there are others which cannot lightly be set aside. I will consider three of these.

Bernardino Realino was an Italian who died in 1616 and whose beatification proceedings began five years later. Witnesses spoke on oath. A gentleman of good standing gave evidence that he had come to see the Father and, finding his door closed, had waited for some time outside. But the door was not completely shut and he noticed an extraordinary radiance streaming through the chinks, which made him wonder why a fire had been lit at midday in April. Pushing open the door he found that the stream of light was emanating from Fr Bernardino, who was kneeling rapt in ecstasy and raised from the floor. The man sat down outside the door, amazed at the light which came through the crannies, before he returned home. In his deposition he said that he had asked himself whether the radiance was due to his imagination, or whether it was the reflection of sunlight, but he remained totally convinced that he had seen real light streaming from the holy man. Under close cross-examination, he could not be shaken in his testimony. He was not alone. A number of people bore testimony of the amazing radiance with which Fr Bernardino's face was at times transformed. Some said that sparks seemed to come from all over his body; others said that they could not recognize all the features of his face because of the intensity of light which came from him. Another witness said he came to see him in the early morning, and found him on his knees, and his face so radiant that it lit up the darkness of the room where he was, despite the shutters being closed (Thurston, 1952: pp. 164f.). The evidence for luminosity here is very strong.

Francis Suarez was a great theologian. A distinguished visitor one afternoon wished to see him. Although there was a stick across his door showing that he did not wish to be disturbed, a lay brother did enter to tell him, as he had been instructed to do whenever this visitor called. He found the outer room in darkness with the shutters closed because of the heat.

I called the Father, but he made no answer. As the curtain which shut off his working room was drawn, I saw through the space between the curtain and the jambs of the door a great brightness. I pushed aside the curtain and entered the inner apartment. Then I perceived that a blinding light was coming from the crucifix, so intense that it was like the reflection of the sun from glass windows, and I felt I could not have remained looking at it without being completely blinded. The light streamed from the crucifix upon the face and breast of Father Suarez, and in the brightness I saw him in a kneeling position in front of the crucifix, his head uncovered, his hands joined, and his body in the air lifted five palms from the floor on a level with the table on which the crucifix stood.

The lay brother retired, and when later Suarez questioned him about this, he tried to make him promise to tell no one what he had seen. On the advice of his confessor he drew up a signed statement with the endorsement that it should not be opened until after Suarez' death. Both the lay brother and his confessor were people of acknowledged integrity (Thurston, 1952: p. 166).

St Thomas à Kempis wrote a life of his contemporary and compatriot St Lydwina of Schiedam, who was 'found by her companions to be surrounded by so great a divine brightness that, seeing the splendour and struck by exceeding fear, they dared not approach near her . . . Her cell was so wonderfully flooded by light that to the beholders the cell itself appeared full of material lamps or fires' (Scully, 1912: p. 117). She was also said to be surrounded by a sweet-smelling fragrance, another paranormal phenomenon known as 'the odour of sanctity' (Thurston, 1952: p. 157).

Why this light? It is interesting to note that Prosper Lambertini (Pope Benedict XIV) in his treatise on beatification and canonization did not think that it necessarily had a supernatural cause. He wrote:

It seems to be a fact that there are natural flames which at times visibly encircle the human head, and also that from a man's whole person fire may on occasion radiate naturally, not, however, like a flame which streams upwards, but rather in the form of sparks which are given off all round; further, that some people become resplendent with a blaze of light, though this is not inherent in themselves, but attaches rather

to their clothes, or to the staff or spear which they are carrying. (Lambertini, 1766: iv.i.26)

An attempt was made to solve this mystery by an Italian doctor
in the case of the 'luminous woman' who in 1934 attracted public
attention in the English press, and whose case is quoted by
Fr Thurston (1952: p. 162). The woman in question was religious and had been fasting very strictly in Lent. This had the
effect of increasing the radiant power of her blood. Her breath-
ing and her heartbeats redoubled when the luminous phenomena
appeared and heavy perspiration followed. The doctor held that
the fasting caused an excess of sulphides, which become luminous when excited by the increased ultra-violet radiation. So far
as I know this has never been followed up, and it would be
strange indeed if fasting increased ultra-violet radiation sufficiently to have this effect; and while many people have fasted
strictly, the luminous phenomenon is exceptionally rare. So this
explanation is doubtful. Perhaps the true explanation is very different.

Fr Thurston closes his chapter with words which are worth
quoting:

Let me add that the frequent occurrence of luminous
phenomena in mediumistic séances – many of these being well
attested in circumstances where the strictness of control
seems to preclude the possibility of fraud – strongly inclines
me to believe that similar manifestations are not likely to be
lacking in the records of mysticism. As the wonders of
Pharaoh's magicians followed closely the type of miracles of
Moses and Aaron, so no careful student of psychical research
can fail to notice a very close resemblance between the
marvels recorded in the lives of the Saints, and the phenomena of what is loosely called spiritualism. What the connection

is, I am not here concerned to inquire, nor do I believe that we yet possess data enough to be able to deal adequately with the problem. (Thurston, 1952: p. 170)

No satisfactory explanation has been given of this phenomenon, and given the parallel which Fr Thurston draws between the physical phenomena of saints and the physical phenomena of spiritualism, the luminosity can properly be called paranormal. (The connection between holiness and the paranormal is a fascinating subject but no one has yet explained it.) And if this is what has happened to holy people, is it not reasonable to assume that this accounts for the shining brightness of Jesus at his transfiguration? If there is any explanation, I think it may well lie in the sphere of psychosomatic phenomena. The body is affected by the soul: when the soul is uplifted in ecstasy to God, it can happen that the body too is uplifted in what is known as levitation; when the soul is united to Christ in meditation of his suffering on the Cross, the stigmata may occur; when the soul is refreshed and rendered sweet by the grace of Christ, physical fragrancy may result, which has been noted from the martyrdom of Polycarp onwards; when the soul is inflamed with love towards God, *incendium amoris* may raise the physical temperature of the body. In the same way, it may be that when the soul is incandescent through union with God, it may show itself in luminosity of the body. Even so, the mechanism by which this may happen is completely unknown.

Does such an explanation detract from the theological significance of the transfiguration of Jesus as the Evangelists conceived it? Hardly. The dazzling whiteness of Christ is quite separate from the vision which accompanied it, through which his disciples became aware of his divine sonship. Light in almost all religions is a sign of divinity, as we read in the Prologue to St John's Gospel and as also appears in the Nicene Creed. For Jesus to be associated with light shows his association with God. It is more difficult to associate light with his future parousia, except in so far as he may then show himself literally in his true colours.

Chapter 8

The Feeding of the Multitudes

Mark 6.34–44; Matthew 14.14-41; Luke 9.12–16;
John 6.1–12 (Mark 8.1–10; Matthew 15.32–9)

In all four Gospels there is an account of how Jesus fed five thousand people (according to Matthew, apart from women and children) with a few loaves and fish. According to John, these were contributed by a lad among the company. There is also in St Mark's and St Matthew's Gospels a similar account of Jesus feeding four thousand people, on this occasion from seven loaves (and, Matthew adds, a few small fish). Such was the surplus that there was left enough to fill, in the case of the five thousand, twelve baskets, and, in the case of the four thousand, seven baskets. It seems very likely that these stories were all derived from a single source. There is a proper context for the story in the case of the five thousand. The Twelve had returned from their mission and Jesus saw that they needed refreshment, so he took them away to a desert place; but the crowds followed them there. That was how it came about that a multitude were in the wilderness without food, although it hardly explains how there were containers to hand for all the surplus bread after the meal. There is no such context for the feeding of the four thousand: the setting is vague, with the statement that 'in those days the multitude [was] very great', and we are told that they had been in the wilderness for three days.

Crossan (1991: p. 401) has suggested that Mark deliberately created a doublet of miraculous feeding in order to increase the culpable incomprehension of the disciples, but he gives no reason why the Evangelist should have wanted to do this. However, Mark 8 is clearly another version of Mark 6 and it is very likely that there is a symbolic significance in the two accounts. The numbers present, the amount of food contributed and the amount left over all have symbolic potential, but no one has shown convincingly what the significance is, so it is easy to feel sympathy for the Twelve when they were rebuked by Jesus for their lack of understanding (Mark 8.17). It is often assumed that one feeding is oriented towards the Jews and the other towards Gentiles.

As it stands, the narrative bears some resemblance to the institution of the Eucharist at the Last Supper and it may be for that reason that it has been given such prominence. It could be explained as an anticipation of the Messianic Feast, and therefore a veiled eschatological sacrament (Schweitzer, 1949: p. 377). Certainly, in the Fourth Gospel the feeding is an eschatological sign (John 6.54).

It has been held that the feedings are mythical, based on the miraculous appearance of manna for the Israelites in the wilderness (Exodus 16.14f.), or on the account in 2 Kings 4.42–4, when Elisha was brought twenty loaves of barley and corn on the husk and told his servant to give it to a hundred 'sons of the prophets', and this proved sufficient for them. However, the parallel with manna is very slight (merely that both were food provided in the wilderness) and the numbers in the Kings and Gospel stories are different. It would seem extraordinary that the accounts of the Gospel feedings arose from these Old Testament stories. Other reasons have been given for holding that there is no historical basis for the feedings. Crossan (1991: p. 402) has written:

The bread and the fish Eucharist was originally a post-resurrectional confession of Jesus's continued presence at the ritualised meals of the believing community. Open commensality survived as ritualised meal. Once narrative Gospels were composed that tradition was placed both before the resurrection, in the common source for Mark 6 and John 6, and after the resurrection, in Luke 24 and John 21. Even more fascinating, however, are those fleeting but tantalising glimpses we catch across the bread and fish tradition as it moves from *general commensality* towards *leadership group* and on to *specific leaders*. (His italics)

Possibly the various stories mentioned were influenced by developing trends in pre-narrative Gospel traditions, but it seems strange that, if indeed bread and fish meals do refer solely to Jesus' continued presence with the disciples, they should be placed both before the resurrection and after it. It is easier to explain the feedings, with their multiple attestation, as based on a historical event during the public ministry of Jesus.

The historical circumstances of the feeding have been veiled by the 'spin' that the Evangelists have put on the story. Sufficient of the original account in St John's Gospel and the Synoptics remains to enable us to recover what actually happened. The clue lies in the Johannine account, where we are told that Jesus realized that the multitude had come out into the desert in order to take him by force and make him king (John 6.15); in other words, this was the prelude to a revolt against Rome to install Jesus as Messianic ruler, an attempt which he successfully foiled (Montefiore, 1962: pp. 135–41).

According to Mark, when the apostles returned from their mission the strange phrase 'there were many coming and going' occurs, best interpreted as preparatory arrangements for the impending revolt. Jesus escaped from this bustle with his disciples by boat to a desert place in the wilderness. But their departure was known, people rushed together 'out of all cities' and the great concourse reached Jesus' destination before he did. It was a difficult situation: he had compassion on them because they appeared leaderless; he began to teach them many things, in particular his vision of the kingdom; but they would not listen. Jesus knew he could not be the leader that they wanted. He made them sit down on the green grass – significantly the grass was green only around Passover, when the Messiah was supposed to arrive – in companies of fifty and a hundred (a reference to how military formations gathered from the different cities). Mark emphasizes that all of them were men, who would be the people who would lead an uprising, while Matthew softens it to include women and children. Jesus then fed the multitude and forced the disciples to leave before dismissing the huge crowd. If he were to prevent a Messianic uprising he could trust no one. He departed into the mountainous region to pray alone. Mark very rarely depicts Jesus praying, but this was a critical situation.

Traditionalists have held that this miracle was due to the divine nature of Christ which gave him power to produce bread to feed a multitude. Pope Leo I mentioned it in a missive he wrote to Flavian in the East in AD 449 which has become known as the Tome of Leo. It was regarded in the West as settling the difficult matter of Christ's two natures, and greatly influenced the ecumenical Council of Chalcedon, which produced in AD 551 its famous Definition (Chadwick, 2001: pp. 569ff.). In it Leo wrote: 'To be hungry, to thirst, to grow weary, is evidently human. But to satisfy five thousand men with five loaves . . . is without ambiguity divine.' Without ambiguity? I think not!

More sceptical critics have sought to explain away the miracle of the feeding on the grounds that it was unlikely that Jesus, with his limitations of human nature, had powers of this kind over physical nature. Other commentators have tried to dilute the miracle by supposing that the numbers were far smaller than the Evangelists record; but this hardly accords with the statement that they rushed together from every city. Others suppose that there was no miracle: the people were simply induced to share the unexpired remains of their picnic lunches, in which case why was the story ever remembered and recorded? Others think that the miracle of spiritual food that Jesus gave them became in the course of tradition a miracle of physical feeding. None of these suggestions does justice to the situation: feeding recounted six times in four Gospels must have been of major importance. It could not have developed in any of these ways; and if the reconstruction attempted above holds good, none of these options fits that situation. Attempts at softening the miracle are less credible than its acceptance.

Once again illumination may come by reference to the saints. There is a chapter devoted to the multiplication of food in the book of Fr Thurston which I have cited earlier. It is interesting to note that this is mentioned in the bulls of canonization of saints. Prosper Lambertini (Pope Benedict XIV), in his great treatise on the beatification and canonization of saints (IV.i.23), refers to the miraculous multiplication of food in the bulls of canonization of many well-known saints, mentioning in particular St Clare of Assisi, St Richard of Chichester, St Teresa of Avila, St Frances of Rome, St Mary Magdalen of Pazzi and St Pius V. He refers moreover to other similar cases connected with the names of St Pius Thomas of Villanova, St Lewis Bertrand (the evidence for which Fr Thurston finds in some respects unclear), St Rose of Lima, St Aloysius Gonzala, St Francis Xavier, St Cunegund and St Elizabeth Queen of Portugal.

This is an impressive list, and it must be remembered that the depositions of witnesses for a case of beatification were taken under oath. No doubt many of these cases would be treated with the same scepticism as Jesus' feeding of the multitudes on the far side of the Sea of Galilee. New Testament scholars, especially if not Roman Catholics, are often a little ignorant of the histories of the saints and perhaps doubtful of the sworn testimonies about them; this can at times limit their interpretation of biblical material. No doubt there has sometimes been fraud and gross exaggeration. But, as Prosper Lambertini insisted, proper pre-cautions should be taken against errors of malobservation, etc., and only afterwards should the supernatural implications of these multiplications be fully recognized.

Fr Thurston (1952: pp. 386ff.) has drawn attention in partic-ular to two or three cases. One concerns Andrew Hubert Fournet, the nineteenth-century co-founder of the religious con-gregation Les Filles de la Croix, which was widespread in some countries but hardly known in Britain. Fr Fournet was sanctified in 1933 and in the depositions of witnesses remarkable tributes were paid to his sanctity as well as to favours he was granted. Fr Thurston focuses on the mother house founded in great poverty in La Puye in Western France. Sr Bartholomew, who for thir-teen years had Fr Fournet as her confessor, said in evidence that when at La Puye she was in charge of the granary. Around two hundred sisters from various parts of France were due to gather there, but she told Fr Fournet that there was not enough corn to feed them and no money to buy more. He replied, 'My child, where is your faith?', and climbed up to the granary, walking around two little heaps of grain stored there. Fr Fournet insisted on going ahead with the assembly, and Sr Bartholomew swore that every day she went to the granary to draw the corn that was needed from the beginning of July to the middle of September. When she left to go elsewhere, the two heaps of corn were exactly the same size as when she first showed them to Fr Fournet in the granary.

Sr Mamertus, another nun at La Puye, recounted what happened a year or two later. The nun, who had succeeded Sr Bartholomew in charge of the granary, told her that she did not know what to do as there were only six or eight bushels of corn in the granary. In the absence of the foundress she told Fr Fournet, who said, 'My dear child, how little faith you have!' He made his way to the granary and Sr Mamertus, through the keyhole, saw him kneeling at prayer over the corn. The nun in charge measured the corn later in the day and found there 60 bushels. These depositions were made some time after the events, but they were made on oath by responsible people.

Another case cited by Fr Thurston (1952: p. 389) concerns St Don Bosco. In 1860 he was living in one of the Salesian houses, in Turin, where a good number of students were in training. There was virtually no bread in the house, the baker having refused to provide any more until his bill was paid. There was nothing for breakfast. Don Bosco, emerging from the confessional, ordered the little bread left in the house to be collected and said it would be distributed. A young man who had been making his confession attended closely to what ensued: Don Bosco was holding a basket containing fifteen or twenty rolls at most; there were about three hundred lads there. He watched Don Bosco carefully as he distributed a roll to each of them, and when he ended there was the same number there as when he started, yet no other rolls had been brought and the basket had not been changed. The young man was so impressed that instead of quitting training as he had intended, he stayed and became a Salesian (Lemoyne, n.d.: vol. 2, pp. 459–60).

Naturally it is not possible to make a well-informed, proper judgement about such cases without an examination of the *Summarium* – all evidence deposed in the sanctification process. Fr Thurston gives a list of many others in whose lives multiplication of food has been reported, some of whom are well-known saints. It is hard to resist his conclusion that, 'though the evidence may often be inadequate, [it] cannot lightly be dismissed as a phenomenon belonging merely to the domain of legend' (p. 395).

If multiplication of food did occur, whether in the Gospels or among the saints, is it to be accepted as a supernatural phenomenon, with God directly interfering with the regularities of nature, whether at the behest of Christ or of his saints acting through the grace of Christ? This might seem to be the case, but there is an aspect of Fr Thurston's account that makes one pause before agreeing. He gives instances of the multiplication of food in circumstances where need was not a factor (pp. 391–4). For example, Fr Angiolo Paoli, who died in 1720 and whose *Life* was published in 1756, is not only credited with giving bread to every beggar he met from the scraps he carried about him but also on occasion with producing at will wine and food for a picnic from scant resources.

This might incline one to think that his *Life* is a piece of fiction. But it is attested by well-known people, given an Imprimatur and contains extracts from the *Summarium* of his beatification process. This is not the only case of the alleged multiplication of food in circumstances when need was not paramount.

If such cases be accepted as genuine, I find it impossible to believe that multiplication of food is supernatural. How could God grant such supersession of natural causation for needs which were essentially trivial? If not supernatural, then we have to look for a paranormal explanation, that is to say, not one that implies a direct intervention by God but one that occurs through the working of laws whose mechanism is completely unknown to us. This would apply to the feeding of the multitudes by Jesus in Galilee as well as by those of his later saints.

There is perhaps a faint analogy to these feedings with apports (objects which appear seemingly from nowhere), which are not uncommon accompaniments of psychic phenomena. I will give two contemporary examples. Matthew Manning has been the recipient of a remarkably large range of psychic phenomena, beginning from his days as a schoolboy at Oakham School. Here is a statement by his old headmaster:

Things that happened when Matthew Manning was at Oakham are simply mind-boggling. He must be the most unique boy that I have ever met in twenty-five years as Master and Headmaster. Of course, I am a sceptic about psychic matters, but I know that something quite extraordinary was happening. I bent over backwards not to get involved but I am sure there were paranormal powers at work to produce such mysterious happenings. I personally witnessed none of the happenings but plenty of people in his school house did. I had him under my personal care for about three years and I became very worried about all these happenings. There was never any explanation about how all these disarrangements of dormitories, etc. occurred. Knives, bricks, glass, pebbles and suchlike appeared without any clue as to their origin. And yet nothing appeared to be missing from other parts of the school. The boys who shared Matthew's dormitory and whose bunks moved about were absolutely adamant that it had happened: they were honest and nice boys and I know that they did not tell lies. (Manning, 1991: p. 91)

Another recent instance of apports concerns a project which took place when three members of the Society for Psychical Research co-operated with a group experimenting in psychic matters in Scole, a village near Diss in Norfolk. Between 1995 and 1997 various phenomena took place and various apports appeared. After discussing these, the Scole Report continued:

Rather more impressive from a veridical point of view was an apport which appeared during the same (13 July 1966) sitting in the translucent Pyrex kitchen bowl placed in the séance room table into which on several occasions a light entered and swirled round bright enough to reveal any contents and to make the bowl glow. When the light was turned on we found a screwed up piece of paper in the centre of the bowl. AR opened it carefully and it was found to contain three ammonite shells and some dust, two of the shells being entire, one broken . . . The material was carefully removed and stored and the paper opened up. One side bore scorched marks around a burnt section. The writing was indecipherable. (Scole Report, 1999: p. 282)

Such apports are trivial when placed beside the Gospel story of the food which fed five thousand. However, they do show that the provision of material from nowhere is a well-attested paranormal phenomenon.

Chapter 9

Walking on the Galilean Lake

Mark 6.45–52; Matthew 14.22f.; John 6.16–21

After the feeding of the five thousand, Jesus is recorded as forcing the disciples to get into a boat and to precede him along the lake back to Bethsaida, while he sent away the multitude; and he then made his way up into the hill country to pray. It had been growing late and, when evening came, the disciples were rowing in the middle of the lake. Jesus was alone on the shore. Rowing against the wind, they were in some trouble. At about three o'clock in the morning they saw Jesus coming towards them, and he seemed about to pass them by. They all saw him; according to Mark, they thought they had seen a ghost and cried out. But he told them to cheer up and not to be frightened: 'It's me', he said. That is the story as Mark tells it. In the Fourth Gospel the context is the same and the account similar, with the additional details that they had rowed about 3 or 4 miles when they saw him, and they then received him into the boat. In Matthew there is a strange addition: Peter gets permission to join Jesus on the water. He begins to sink and cries out for help. Jesus gives him a hand and they get into the boat, whereupon the wind drops.

What is the relationship between the accounts in Mark, John and Matthew? The Matthean version has an addition about Peter which seems to be an allegory, showing his impetuousness, his failure and his reinstatement by Jesus; and then all was well.

It is not found in the Marcan and Johannine accounts and may safely be regarded as secondary and unhistorical. Matthew ends with the words: 'Then they that were in the ship worshipped him [Jesus], saying, Of a truth thou art the Son of God' (Matthew 14.33). As Borg (1997: p. 136) has commented: 'Matthew changes the disciples' puzzlement and lack of understanding into an act of Christian adoration and acclamation. Jesus is now worshipped and he is hailed as the Son of God.'

According to the Fourth Gospel, there was something very strange about Jesus being taken on board, because in the Johannine text they immediately reached the land they were heading for; it was as though they were miraculously transported there (John 6.21). This is recounted without comment, and it should also be regarded as secondary, in accordance with the tendency of that Gospel to heighten the supernatural. It also is an allegory of the way in which, without Jesus, the disciples were helpless, but with Jesus all was well. We are left, then, with just the primitive tradition in the Marcan account which is developed in the other two Gospels. Crossan (1991: p. 406) holds that the Marcan account in Mark 6.45ff. is a doublet of Mark 4.36ff.: when Jesus was asleep in a boat in the evening, the wind got up, he was awakened and the storm abated. There is no good reason for this identification, as the two stories are very different, apart from the fact that in both cases the disciples were in a boat on a windy night, something which must have happened to them not infrequently during Jesus' ministry on the shores of Lake Galilee.

Many critics cannot accept the Marcan story as recording a supernatural event. Bultmann (1931) calls it a miracle story. Dibelius (1934) classifies it as one of the *Novellen*, showing an epiphany of the divine wonder-worker – God who is master of the waves is manifesting his power. Some think that it is a story about the risen Christ which has been attached to the feeding of the five thousand. Others think of it as an allegory of the risen

Jesus coming to rescue his followers as they find themselves in dark times and in a sea of troubles (though there is no hint in the story that the disciples were actually in any danger). It may well have been included in the Marcan collection of stories because of its message of hope in difficult times, but that in itself does not demonstrate that it does not have a historical basis. Some of those who agree that the story has a factual basis have supposed that what actually happened was that the rowers saw Jesus walking along the seashore, and with the surf breaking on a dark night they supposed him to be walking on the waters; the story developed from this misapprehension. It is true that in the Marcan account the text could be understood in the sense of Jesus walking *by* the sea rather than *on* the sea, but this sense was clearly not that intended by the Evangelist. This could be what might have happened during daylight, but at night they would surely have been too far out from the shore to identify anyone walking along it; it is, after all, very improbable that anyone would mistake a person walking along a beach to be walking on water. They would have needed to see water behind him as well as in front of him for that. Furthermore, if Jesus had gone up into the hill country to pray it is more than odd to find him walking along the shore of the lake in the middle of the night.

It has been suggested that this is a post-resurrection story transposed into the earthly ministry of Jesus, but why? Again, it has been thought to have been developed from Old Testament texts, such as Job 9.8. But the reference here to God 'treading on the crests of the waves' is no theophany, and in any case it is translated in the New English Bible as he who 'trod on the sea-monster's back'. There is no way in which the story could have developed from that, and the same could be said of other references, such as Isaiah 51.9f., Habakkuk 3.15 and Psalm 77.19. It is true that the story has nothing to do with the Kingdom of God, and the event did not help anyone in dire need (Meier,

1991: vol. 2, p. 920); but the fact that the story exists in both John and the Synoptics gives it (like the feeding of the multitude) double attestation, and the context is the same in all three Gospels.

If one is left with the possibility that Jesus *was* seen to be walking on the waters of the Sea of Galilee, how can this be accounted for? Was it a supernatural event? The earliest tradition, as found in St Mark's Gospel, does not suggest this as do the Matthean and Johannine accounts; Mark simply records that the disciples were scared by what they saw (Mark 5.50). Was it a mass hallucination of the Twelve? Mass hallucinations are extremely rare.

There is another explanation, which accords well with Mark's remark that the disciples thought they had seen a ghost. It is possible for a holy person with paranormal gifts to concentrate on people in a distant scene to such an extent that they visibly appear to them, speaking to them telepathically. This is called 'bilocation'. It is rare, but there is evidence that it has happened.

A recent case serves as a good example of bilocation. Father Francesco Forgione, born at Pietrelcina near Naples in the nineteenth century, and who died in 1968, is better known as Padre Pio. His process of sanctification, after some years in abeyance, has recently been completed and in June 2002 he was declared a saint. A person of outstanding spirituality, one of only two males to have received the stigmata and renowned for the 'odour of sanctity', he had many paranormal gifts. He had great gifts of healing; he had telepathic insight into the souls of people so that thousands flocked to his confessional; he had the very rare gift of bilocation. Macaffery, a former Director of the British Institute in Florence and, during the Second World War, Chief of Special Operations Europe, became a friend of Padre Pio. The Capuchin Superior of the monastery where Padre Pio lived told him that 'he was appearing all over the place' (Macaffery, 1978: p. 25). In his book Macaffery gives accounts of Padre Pio's bilocation, but he is careful to restrict himself to recounting only what happened to people personally known to him. 'They have been written from memory. It is therefore possible, because of the passage of time, that where there is not direct personal experience, there may be circumstantial details which are not completely accurate; but for the factual occurrence of all the events and episodes herein recounted I can vouch absolutely' (p. vi). There are also

> scores of testimonies from people who claimed on meeting him that they had encountered him before – on a sickbed, on a battlefield, in a church confessional or in a dream . . . When he was challenged as to his awareness of these episodes he would invariably wink and quip cryptically, 'Oh, these little visions and voices.' (Cornford, 1991: p. 276)

Cornford continues:

> A brother monk claimed that Padre Pio had come to him when he was in hospital and healed him of a fatal illness, although it was known that Padre Pio had not been out of his monastery. When his Superior asked him whether he had bilocated, Pio said, 'Is there any doubt about it? Yes, I went, but do not say anything to anyone.'

It is typical of holy people that when strange things happen to them, they do not want it to be known.

If Padre Pio had the gift of bilocation – and the evidence for this is very strong – and if Jesus also had paranormal gifts, he too might have had the gift of bilocation. It is entirely possible that when the disciples saw Jesus walking on the water towards them,

Jesus was bilocating. It cannot be proven and remains a hypothesis; but it seems to me the most likely explanation of the strange Marcan account.

Chapter 10

Return to Earth?

In the last two verses of the Hebrew Bible there is this prophecy of Malachi: 'Behold, I will send you Elijah the prophet before the coming of the great and dreadful day of the LORD; and he shall turn the heart of the fathers to the children, and the heart of the children to their fathers, lest I come and smite the earth with a curse' (Malachi 4.5f.). In other words, Elijah will return to put things right before the end of the world.

Jesus lived in turbulent times with the Holy Land under Roman occupation, and there was a certain expectancy that the Day of the Lord might soon be arriving. People set themselves up as Messiah. According to St John's Gospel (2.19–27), a deputation of priests and Levites arrived from Jerusalem to the place where John the Baptist was baptizing at Bethabara beyond Jordan. The first question they asked him was: 'Are you Elijah?' When he denied this, they asked him whether he was the prophet promised by Moses who would be like himself (Deuteronomy 18.18). Having denied this too, he applied to himself the prophecy of Isaiah (40.3), 'Make straight the way of the Lord' insisting that he was sent to prepare for the Messiah (John 1.26).

It is recorded that the disciples at one point were asking Jesus why the scribes said Elijah must come first, presumably meaning why he must come before the Day of the Lord as prophesied by

Malachi. According to both Mark and Matthew, Jesus replied: 'Elijah does come first to restore all things', and 'they did to him whatever they pleased' (Mark 9.12–13; Matthew 17.12). Mark adds 'as it is written of him', presumably a reference to Malachi. Jesus pointed to his own coming as the Day of the Lord and to John's ministry as that of Elijah who had to prepare his way.

Jesus did not deny that John was preparing the way, but he did contradict John's denial that he was Elijah. Although this incident may well have been misplaced, it seems unlikely that it is entirely unhistorical, because of the other references to John as Elijah come to life again in the teaching of Jesus.

So Jesus believed that John was Elijah and this is not the only occasion on which he made this equation. There is a collection of sayings about the Baptist in Matthew 11, among which Jesus is recorded as saying: 'All the prophets and the law prophesied until John, and if you are willing to accept it, he is Elijah who is to come' (Matthew 11.14). Jesus did not say that John was the way that Malachi's prophecy about the coming of Elijah was fulfilled; he did not say that John spoke in the spirit of Elijah. He said he *was* Elijah and 'There is no reason to doubt that the main point, viz. the identification of the Baptist with Elijah, goes back to and rests upon an authentic saying of our Lord' (Rawlinson, 1949: p. 121). Elijah was believed to have ascended into heaven in a chariot of fire, and presumably was believed to be in heaven, awaiting his return to earth at the Last Day. So how could Jesus identify the two? According to Luke, Jesus' mother Mary was a cousin of John's mother, Elizabeth, who was said to have conceived John in her old age (Luke 1.36). The two women knew each other and, according to Luke, Mary stayed with Elizabeth for three months during her pregnancy. Not only were the two mothers well acquainted, but it seems from St John's Gospel that Jesus had originally been a member of John's company when he began his ministry of baptism and repentance before Jesus started his own mission (John 3.23–6). If we hold that these accounts are founded on historical events, Jesus must have known John well, and (if we may trust Luke) he knew too his mother and his father, and probably the circumstance of John's birth. How then was it possible for him not merely to regard John as fulfilling a prophecy about Elijah but also to *equate* John with Elijah? If this question has been correctly posed, it can be answered only on the assumption that Elijah had returned to earth in the person of John. There is indeed a certain similarity in their characters.

This resembles reincarnation, although that word has Eastern associations foreign to Jewish thought. It is unlikely that Jews in the time of Jesus generally believed in reincarnation, unless the pseudepigraphical writings of the time were meant to be understood in this sense. We have to wait until the days of the Zohar for explicit belief in reincarnation. But it does seem likely from these passages about Elijah that Jews of Jesus' day did hold that certain persons might return to earth in the guise of another person. For this equation of John with Elijah is not the only instance of this kind of identification. According to all three Synoptic Gospels, when Jesus inquired of his disciples near Caesarea Philippi who people said that he was, they answered that some said he was John the Baptist (John by then had been executed and all three Synoptics inform us that Herod too thought that Jesus was exercising John's powers); others said he was Elijah; others said one of the prophets (among whom Matthew identifies Jeremiah). It follows from this that Jesus himself was thought by some to be Elijah, and that people had no difficulty in thinking of prophets as living a second existence in another personality. Commentators, however, fight shy of this seemingly heterodox conclusion, and most of them do not even comment on what must be the plain meaning of Jesus' words.

We certainly do not find elsewhere in the extant literature of Judaism of Jesus' time an explicit belief of any kind of reincarnation. Has this, perhaps, been excised from the records? Josephus recounts that the Essenes believed that the body is a prison house of the soul (*Jewish War* 2.7.11); if it were not for him we would not have known about this. If such a most un-Jewish belief was held by one of the stricter sects of the Jews, it is not impossible that other Jews may have held that prophets could be reincarnated.

Of course when Jesus equated John and Elijah he may have meant only that he was fulfilling the role that had been prophesied about Elijah. However, that is not what is reported to have been said, namely that John was Elijah; and if this is true, it can only be accounted for by a kind of metempsychosis. Reincarnation can hardly be called a natural process; in that sense it can rightly be called paranormal, if it occurs.

But does it occur? Half of the world believes that it does, but this belief has not been endorsed by Christianity, partly because it has been identified with the pagan belief systems of Eastern religions, and partly because, if souls do return to earth, this has been held to detract from Christian hope. (In fact a belief in reincarnation need not be held in Buddhist or Hindu form: it could apply only to persons who need to return to further God's plan for the world, or to people, especially children who die young from illness or violence, who need a further opportunity to mature. Reincarnation need not be thought of as an endless process until nirvana is reached.)

The scientific evidence for reincarnation is not conclusive but it is quite strong. It comes not from dreams and feelings of *déjà vu*, nor from accounts narrated while under hypnosis (e.g. those stories contained in the Bloxham tapes), but from 2,500 alleged cases which have been investigated by Professor Stevenson of the University of Virginia (Stevenson, 1987), selections from which he has published from various cultures – India (1975), Sri Lanka (1977), Turkey and Lebanon (1980), Burma and Thailand (1983); from Tlingit Indians of South East Alaska (1966) and the

Igbo of Nigeria (1986). These come mostly from cultures where there is general acceptance of reincarnation, but Professor Stevenson has also published European cases of the reincarnation type (2003). Here the evidence is less widespread, but this may be because young children have been told by their parents to stop talking about something so alien.

The evidence comes from children between three and eight who remember past lives and give evidence of behavioural memories (when children behave in ways appropriate to an alleged former existence but inappropriate to their present situation), visual images and mental memories of an earlier existence. (After that age memories of a former life tend to die away, in a similar way to other childhood memories.) The children speak with a certitude and intensity which may astonish adults who hear them. They sometimes have knowledge of an alleged former domicile unknown to family members to which they say they used to belong – knowledge that could hardly come from them telepathically. They may conceive hatefulness and a feeling of vengeance against those whom they say murdered them in a previous existence.

It is always necessary to consider alternative explanations: whether there is fraud, telepathy, mistaken memories of what the children have said, or simple coincidence. But Professor Stevenson has gone about his researches with academic thoroughness, giving case histories which list the persons engaged in the investigation, the relevant facts of geography and the possibilities of normal communication between the two families concerned. He gives an account of the life and death of the person the child claims to have been in a former life. He then records statements and recognitions made by the child concerned, and with each statement is given the name of the informant, verification, comments and the time lag between when the statements were made and when they were recorded. He considers the attitude of the parents of both families towards the child's allegations, and even the relevance of any birthmarks to the death or physique of the alleged person of an earlier existence. As a result of this rigorous research it is hard to resist the conclusion that there is a possibility, even a probability, that reincarnation can give the best explanation of children's memories of a former life.

If, after an evaluation of evidence such as Professor Stevenson has produced, reincarnation is considered to be a probability, then it becomes less incredible that John the Baptist, whose character was in many ways similar to that of Elijah, may in fact have been his reincarnation, as Jesus seems to have asserted.

Chapter 11

Healings

The four Gospels all contain accounts of wonderful healings by Jesus during his public ministry. There can be little doubt that Jesus did perform healings in a way that astonished people. How else, in an age when there was no mass communication, could he have attracted such a large following during his public ministry, which lasted at most for three years, and possibly for only a single year? Furthermore, the fact that Jesus 'wrought remarkable deeds' is attested not only in Christian writings but also in Josephus' *Antiquities* (18.63f.), if we may conclude that Josephus did indeed mention Jesus and that Agapius' Arabic version of it is likely to have been what Josephus wrote (Pines, 1971: p. 70).

How did Jesus heal people? With someone like the paralytic let down through the roof of a house, he intuited that a spiritual paralysis was inducing physical paralysis. Again, it is well known that some skin diseases are caused by stress, and it is possible that those who are said to have been lepers – it is uncertain exactly what was meant by the Greek word used here – may have been cured through his positive words and through their faith. More than once the words 'Your faith has made you whole' are found in the Gospels, and presumably Jesus meant what he said. Usually he needed the co-operation of the person he healed: 'Do you really want to be healed?' he asked on more than one occasion, although when he healed at a distance he only had the co-operation of those who came to ask for his help.

But it would be idle to suggest that all Jesus' healings were of this kind.

It was commonly believed in the first century BC that illness was caused by demons, and one of the reasons for the early success of the Christian religion was the belief that Jesus conquered the demons. So it is perhaps natural, if Jesus shared the human nature of his day, that he should have used exorcism in his cure of the sick, and through his magnetic personality the person was healed. Occasionally perhaps, as in the case of the demoniac in the tombs, a man was literally possessed, but possession is a highly unusual occurrence: the Church today has to rule out all other causes for mental sickness before an exorcism can be authorized, and that very rarely indeed.

Jesus used other means of healing. Sometimes he simply spoke an authoritative word. Often he used the laying on of hands. He said that a serious case of epilepsy could only be healed after prayer. On one occasion a woman with a persistent gynaecological disorder was cured simply by touching him. There were other healers, including healers in the pagan world such as Apollonius of Tyana (Eels, 1923: 4.45), and there is no good reason to think that Jesus was the only person who could heal people when all other attempted remedies had failed. Since Jesus' day there have been many remarkable cases of healing, in some cases instant healing, brought about through the ministry of the Church, either sacramentally through unction or the laying on of hands, through meditation and contemplation, through intercessory prayer, or through people with special gifts of healing, some of whom have been authorized to carry out their ministry in the Church. In the twentieth century the churches rediscovered the ministry of healing and many books have been written on the subject.

The human body has such a large variation in its reaction to disease and illness that it is difficult to pinpoint a particular reason for a sudden cure. Positive reaction to a placebo illustrates how mysterious recovery of health may be. A growing body of research is linking psychological influences to the immune system's functioning, although this is mostly concerned with psychological stress leading to illness. The study of religious involvement and the immune system is in its infancy but there is some evidence to show that stress causes increase of cortisol, which results in dampening the immune system, while religious experience can have the opposite effect (Koenig et al., 2001: pp. 288f.). However, it is improbable that this could have been the cause of the immediate healings recorded in the Gospels.

Human beings are psychosomatic – the body is closely meshed with the soul. No one quite knows the relationship between the two. It seems incontrovertible that some people do have a special gift of healing, and this does not necessarily depend on their religious convictions. A Federation of Spiritual Healers exists, to which non-religious practitioners may belong. I do not refer here to those popular Protestant preachers who in large gatherings make extravagant claims of healing which often do little more than temporarily relieve pain, but to those who quietly exercise their gift of healing without advertisement for the permanent benefit of the sick.

There are individual healers too. I give an example here of one. Matthew Manning has a remarkable record of curing or alleviating a large range of illnesses including cancer. I mention him for a particular reason: he is the only person (known to me) about whom serious attempts have been made to discover the way in which his paranormal gifts work. As a schoolboy and a young man, Manning exercised many paranormal gifts, but he became convinced that his life's work lay in helping sick people, and he now practises healing, both in groups, by simply concentrating on an individual or by the laying on of hands.

In his younger days Manning attended a conference of scientists in Ottawa where an electroencephalograph (EEG) was attached to his scalp by means of electrodes through which readings were taken when he was bending metals. An Oxford professor (incidentally a Nobel laureate) was present. The distribution of power in his EEG spectrum when he was attempting to bend metal was quite different from when he was resting or talking. His concentration of energy in the Theta band is rarely seen when people are in a waking state. Further tests later located the source of this energy in the limbic system of the brain. Kirlian photographs showed a halo round his fingertips which was much stronger when he was undertaking paranormal activity than when he was at rest (Manning, 1974: pp. 57–60). Presumably similar results would be found in his later healing sessions.

Later, photographs taken with a Polaroid camera by a former Fellow of Trinity College, Cambridge, showed bright light around him when he was concentrating on the paranormal, and further photographs taken when he was concentrating on another person showed bright circles of light around her head (Manning, 1974: pp. 128f.). It may be presumed that when Manning was undertaking healing there would be similar results; but of course it would be pastorally inappropriate to take readings and photographs in such situations.

Whether this is the mode of all paranormal healing it is not possible to say. This gift of healing can be exercised by persons who are not themselves religious. But there is a curious connection between paranormal gifts and mysticism and sanctity. Did Jesus also have this kind of healing energy and, in view of his sanctity, did he have it in pre-eminent degree? If he did, he would surely have used this in the healings that he carried out, either when he laid hands on people, or when he was simply concentrating on a person. This is not to say that some of his healings were not, properly speaking, spiritual healings, and as he said of the epileptic boy when he came down from the Mount of Transfiguration, some kinds of illness can only be healed by prayer.

Similarly, the healings allegedly carried out through the interces-
sion of the saints, even resulting in inexplicable changes in the
human body, can hardly be explained on a paranormal hypothesis,
but seem to be the result of some deeper, spiritual activity. This
does not overturn the view that some healings of Jesus, previously
considered supernatural, may derive from a healing energy
emanating from certain gifted people in a way that has proved
inexplicable to science and which is paranormal in nature.

Chapter 12

Resurrection Appearances

Without belief in the resurrection of Jesus, the Christian religion would never have come into being. This belief was based on the resurrection appearances of Jesus, the empty tomb and the experience of the risen Christ in the hearts of believers. In this chapter I will consider only the nature of the resurrection appearances of Jesus as recounted in the Gospels.

What is to be made of the resurrection appearances of Jesus? The evidence that his disciples believed that they saw and spoke with him after his death is overwhelming. But what did they see? Did they see him in his old earthly body, so that either he never really died or he was miraculously resuscitated after two days in the tomb? But earthly bodies decay after death and in any case they do not go through closed doors. Was he in a kind of 'interim body' after his earthly body had died and before he ascended into heaven in his glorified body? But we know nothing of any such 'interim body'. Or did a myth of Jesus' resurrection grow up after his death in such a way that it gave rise to resurrection stories? Paul, though, went to Jerusalem and saw Peter within three years of his conversion, and both fervently believed that Jesus had really risen from the dead, so there would not have been time for such a myth to arise. Or was the vision which the disciples saw a purely subjective vision, the mere product of their imagination? This does not seem very likely, as they had fled at his arrest, and they had no expectation of his resurrection. Indeed they were downcast at what seemed the total failure of all their hopes and the end of Jesus' mission.

Another possibility would be that the disciples' vision of the risen Jesus was a 'veridical hallucination' – that is to say, a hallucination in so far as it was the product of those parts of the brain which give rise to sight and hearing, but veridical in the sense that what they experienced was caused by the actual presence of the risen Jesus who was in communication with them, this being the only mode by which he could make known his spiritual presence in a way that would thoroughly convince his disciples that he was alive. Some such theory has been suggested by Renan (1863), Kirsopp Lake (1907), Emmet (1909), Streeter (1912), Cadoux (1941) and Perry (1959). There must have been some element of hallucination in what the disciples saw, because they did not see a naked Jesus who had left his grave clothes behind in the tomb, but one clothed as he usually had been, a detail which must have been subjectively added. On the other hand, the spiritual presence of Jesus was real because this alone could have changed their depressed spirits after his death on the cross into the joy, happiness and enthusiasm they felt when they saw their risen Lord.

Hallucinations are of different kinds: some are physiological in origin, caused by sensory deprivation, fasting, brain disease, *delirium tremens*, or delirium caused by hysteria or schizophrenia. There have been attempted neurological explanations of religious visions, such as lesions of the temporal lobe of the brain or cortical disinhibition in which fantasies turn into hallucinations (Wiebe, 1997: pp. 172ff.). No evidence has been put forward sufficient to validate such theories. Attempts have also been made to explain religious hallucinations as a result of wish-fulfilment or stress, although again no evidence has been produced to prove this.

Just what are visual hallucinations?

These may be defined as perceptions in the absence of a visual stimulus. It is common to find that objects and people in a hallucinatory episode are somewhat distorted, being for example much smaller (micropsia) or much larger (macropsia) than in real life. But otherwise their hallmark is that of a visually normal scene, indeed one that is commonly, though not always, reported as a pleasant one . . . They are commonly in vivid colours. Their normality is such that Aldous Huxley wrote, 'there can be no doubt that exactly those parts of [the] retina which could be affected by the image of a cat . . . or the portions of the sensorium with which those organs of sense are connected, are thrown into a corresponding state of activity by some internal cause.' Hallucinations, like dreams, are therefore *visually normal*.

The visual normality of dreams and hallucinations and impression of reality that accompanies them are so intense and compelling that all of us have experienced situations which we subsequently find difficult to ascribe to dreams or imagination. It is difficult not to conceive them as internally generated images which are fed back into the cortex as if they were coming from outside. If this were so, one would naturally expect that the primary visual cortex might be involved, if only because in normal vision signals enter in area VI in the visual areas of the striate cortex. Indeed evidence suggests that during dreaming there is a massive increase in cerebral blood flow not only in the visual area of the pre-striate cortex, but also in the striate cortex itself. (Zeki, 1993: p. 326)

Such are normal hallucinations. But veridical hallucination belongs to a different genre. The word 'veridical' means truthful, and for a hallucination of someone to be truthful there must be genuine contact between two persons, even though both are not physically present at the time when it takes place. The most probable explanation of this phenomenon was first made by Frederick Myers (1919: p. 191) who held that one person became aware of another person's condition or situation by means of telepathy and this is communicated to the conscious mind in a visual form in which a percipient contributes something from his or her knowledge of that person.

Veridical hallucinations of the living can occur, as in a well-attested case when a young girl who had gone out for a walk saw her mother lying in her bedroom and rushed home to find a doctor who managed to save her life after a heart attack. Many instances can also be given of hallucinations, not only of the living (Gurney et al., 1918) but also after death, when someone sees another person without knowing that they have recently died.

Here is an example:

The percipient's half brother (whom she called her brother) had been shot down in France on the nineteenth of March 1917. She herself was in India. 'My brother', she said, 'appeared to me on the nineteenth of March 1917. At the time I was either sewing or talking to my baby – I cannot quite remember what I was doing at that moment. The baby was on the bed. I had a very strong feeling that I must turn round. On doing so, I saw my brother, Eldred Bowyer-Bowyer. Thinking he was alive and had been sent out to India I was simply delighted to see him and turned round quickly to put the baby in a safe place; and then turned again and put my hand out to him when I found he was not there. I thought he was only joking and looked everywhere. It was only when I couldn't find him that I became very frightened and [had] the awful fear [that] he might be dead . . . Two weeks later I saw in the paper that he was missing.' (Tyrrell, 1953: p. 37)

Here is another case:

Shortly after my wife had been confined of my second daughter, about the end of September 1880, my wife informed me that she had seen Ackhurst about one in the morning. I of course told her that it was nonsense, but she persisted and said that he had appeared to her with only his trousers and a shirt on, and the remark she made was that he was dressed just as she had seen him in *Corsican Brothers* (he was an actor). I tried to persuade her that it was a dream, but she insisted it was an apparition. As near as I can remember, about six months later, I met a mutual friend of Ackhurst and of mine. He said, 'Do you know that he is dead?' I said, 'No. When did he die?' He said, 'I don't know the exact date but it was about six months ago', and he further told me that it was at about one o'clock in the morning. (Gurney, 1989: p. 411)

Clearly the resurrection stories in the Gospels differ markedly in some respects from these stories. These veridical hallucinations, known as 'crisis appearances', emerge within twelve hours of a death, whereas the resurrection appearances took place over a period of forty days (unless the author of St Luke's Gospel regarded that as a convenient round number).

The appearances were not concerned with the death of Jesus but they were appearances of the risen Jesus. The likenesses between crisis appearances and resurrection appearances could suggest, however, that it is not impossible that Jesus used the same paranormal means by which a recently dead person was able to communicate with friends and relations in order to communicate with his disciples and to show that he had not only died but was alive.

If this is so and the resurrection appearances of Jesus were indeed veridical hallucinations, they were truthful representations of his spiritual presence in a visual form. They were veridi-cal because the risen Christ really was spiritually present. The images formed were not internally generated, as in other kinds of hallucination, but they were transferred to the brain by a form of telepathy. They were not 'internally generated images which are fed back into the cortex as if they were coming from outside'. They came from outside, not in the usual manner by which we can see things but by means of a kind of telepathy; and while, as we have seen in Chapter 4, most people agree that telepathy does exist, we do not know the mechanism by which it works. (Incidentally, the visions which Jesus had at his baptism and transfiguration may well have been generated by not dissimilar means, that is to say, fed into the cortex from outside by a process similar to telepathy.)

If the resurrection appearances can be explained in this way, they provide veridical (truthful) knowledge of Jesus' life after death. As we have seen, hallucinations are generally indistin-guishable from our normal vision of objective people and objects. If Jesus appeared to his disciples in this way when the last thing that they expected was to see him, of course they were filled with joy and could hardly believe the evidence of their eyes, so they did not always immediately recognize him. What could have been a better way for him to communicate his presence to them? His earthly body seems to have dematerialized, and earthly bodies are the only kind of bodies of which we know and which we can see. So he used a means similar to telepathy to assure them of his presence, through veridical hallucination; and he communicated telepathically by words as well in order to give them orders. For his quasi-telepathic communication with them resulted not merely in visual presence but also in speech.

A further difference between resurrection appearances and 'crisis appearances' is that Jesus appeared to more than one person at once; to groups of the disciples and, on one occasion according to Paul, to five hundred at once (1 Corinthians 15.6). Again, he was not always immediately recognized (e.g. by Mary of Magdala [John 20.15] and the two disciples on the way to Emmaus [Luke 24.16]). Further, the extended conversation between the risen Jesus and his disciples is altogether exceptional. However, exceptional characteristics are only to be expected in this altogether extraordinary use of veridical hallucination: indeed it could be said that veridical hallucinations only give us some kind of analogy of what happened in the case of Jesus' resurrection appearances.

There are also similarities. Phantasms of the dead appear only to people who have had emotional ties with them and it has often been noticed that Jesus appeared only to his disciples and friends and family. Phantasms are not constricted by physical objects and Jesus appeared to go through doors. Phantasms seldom allow themselves to be touched and Jesus did not want to be touched by Mary of Magdala (John 20.17). It is true that, according to Matthew 28.9, the disciples 'held him by his feet' as they worshipped him, but most commentators regard this particular appearance as secondary.

Professor C. H. Dodd, who subjected the resurrection stories to form–critical analysis, found two main types (Dodd, 1955: pp. 9ff.). One was a concise narrative rather like a pronouncement story, consisting of the situation, the appearance of Jesus, the greeting, recognition and the word of command. Of such a kind are Matthew 28.8–10 (the women on the way from the tomb), Matthew 28.18–20 (the eleven disciples on a mountain in Galilee) and John 20.19–21 (late on Sunday evening when the doors were shut). These encounters are consonant with the hypothesis of veridical hallucination.

The second class of story is much lengthier and more detailed; tales told with all the skill of the narrator and therefore lending themselves to improvement in the telling. One such story is

Luke 24.13–32, the journey of two disciples to Emmaus with an unknown traveller, who turned out to have been Jesus and who made himself known to them in the breaking of bread, at which instant he vanished. The story is used to illustrate the importance of Old Testament testimonies to Jesus, with flashbacks to the empty tomb, and leads up to Jesus having appeared to Simon. There is also a probable reference to his Eucharistic presence in the reference to the breaking of bread. It seems probable that a storyteller has been at work on an original appearance of Jesus, the exact details of which it is hard now to discover.

The same kind of comment can be made about John 21.1–13, the appearance of the risen Jesus to the disciples after they had spent a night fishing on the Sea of Galilee when Jesus invited them to join him for breakfast. Here again the story is told in dramatic detail including the exact number of fish caught, and it would seem that the storyteller has been at work. The essence of the story is the appearance of the risen Jesus to the disciples on the shore of the Sea of Galilee. Here too there is a Eucharistic overtone in Jesus taking bread and giving it to the disciples. The story provides a setting for Jesus' commission to Peter. It has many details in common with Luke 5.1–11, when Jesus directed the disciples to a huge shoal of fish, and I have earlier suggested that that was its original setting. Here it is part of an appendix to the Fourth Gospel; the Gospel of St John originally ended at John 20.

In Professor Dodd's analysis there are three stories which do not fit into either of these two classes. One is the appearance of the risen Jesus to the eleven and those with them in Luke 24.36–49. They were terrified and thought they were seeing a ghost. Jesus tried to convince them, first by telling them to feel him, and second by eating some fish and honey. The story starts as a simple resurrection encounter but has been worked over to produce 'a piece of controversial apologetic set in the framework of such a story' (Dodd, 1955: p. 17). It seems remote from the original tradition and, apart from the appearance of the risen Jesus, its details cannot be taken as authentic.

The second story is John's account of Mary of Magdala's encounter with the risen Jesus (John 20.11–17). This has poignant details, but in essence it contains the familiar pattern of Jesus' presence, her recognition of him and the command which he gives her. Either it is brilliantly written out of the writer's imagination or it contains, in his own inimitable style, the story of Mary, who had recounted what actually occurred. The additional details in no way detract from the simple pattern of a recognition story, and for this reason it may be regarded as historically based.

The third resurrection story is John 20.26–9, the story of doubting Thomas' encounter with the risen Jesus, after having been absent when he appeared to the disciples the previous Sunday evening. It follows on from that earlier encounter and indeed cannot be understood without it. The account of Thomas being invited to feel Jesus' hands and side has an obviously apologetic motif, evoking from Thomas the words, 'My Lord and my God', the only time that Jesus is plainly called God in all four Gospels and a statement which forms the climax of that Gospel. It leads on to the words attributed to Jesus: 'Blessed are those who have not seen and yet have believed', and the final words of the chapter: 'These are written that you might believe that Jesus is the Christ, the Son of God, and believing may have life in his name.' (John 21, the appendix containing the account of the huge catch of fish and Simon's commission, must have been added later.) The apologetic note makes its testimony unsafe. It is interesting that the stories in which the risen Jesus eats food all seem to be written for apologetic reasons and doubt must be raised about their historicity.

Just as important as the resurrection stories are the lists of those to whom the risen Jesus appeared (Acts 1.3f.; 1 Corinthians 15.3–8; Luke 24.34). As for the stories, a consideration of their form leads to the conclusion that the risen Jesus did indeed appear to the disciples, but not all the stories about his appearances can be taken *au pied de la lettre*. It is noteworthy that the stories of Jesus' resurrection appearances cannot be paralleled by analogies from other fields.

There is no single appearance that is common to any two Gospels. Mark has no appearances if we disregard its 'longer ending' and consider it a pastiche made out of the other stories. Matthew has appearances in Galilee, Luke in Jerusalem and John in both. But we have seen reason to doubt whether John's account of the risen Jesus on the shore of the Lake of Galilee is rightly placed here as a resurrection story. How are we to reconcile these different locales? We may disregard the Lucan saying that the disciples are to remain in Jerusalem until they are clothed with power from on high, for his plan of Gospel and Acts marks two stages of the gospel, from Galilee to Jerusalem and from Jerusalem to Rome; and if this is to be fulfilled, it follows that the disciples must remain in Jerusalem after the resurrection from Passover to Pentecost. If this veto may be disregarded, it is possible, just, to reconcile encounters in both Galilee and Jerusalem. But, as we have seen, that does not mean that all the resurrection stories deserve to be equally regarded as authentic: naturally, the needs and circumstances of the early Church have affected them.

Having concluded that the disciples did indeed see the risen Jesus, we are forced back on the question asked throughout this book: was this a purely supernatural event or did it make use of the paranormal phenomenon of veridical hallucination? It is noteworthy that there is no mention of the supernatural in the Gospel accounts of the resurrection stories, and a paranormal explanation is consistent with a critical examination of their contents.

Epilogue

There are four kinds of objections to what I have written in this book. In the first place I have argued that the attempt to find historical events and actual sayings in the Gospels is not fruitless: there will be no certainties, but some sayings or events will satisfy the necessary criteria for historicity far better than others, and these will have a high probability of recounting accurately what was said or what happened. Those who do not accept this will regard this study as a waste of time.

Second, I have attempted to show that parapsychology is not a bogus enterprise, but it is a study in which scholars may properly engage. There are those who hold that there are no such things as paranormal phenomena or paranormal powers, and they conclude that those who claim that these do exist are either mistaken or fraudulent. Naturally, those who hold such views will regard this study as worthless.

Third, some will hold that all the passages considered in this study in which paranormal powers are suggested can be better explained as miraculous events of which God is the direct author. Others will contend that these passages have developed as myths in order to emphasize the divine nature of Jesus. Neither will see any real value in this study.

Fourth, there will be those who accept the possibility that Jesus had paranormal powers, but they will not think that the case for them has been successfully argued here.

Naturally, I would not have undertaken the study unless I believed that it is possible to find historicity in events and sayings in the Gospels, that parapsychology should be accepted as a discipline in which scholars may properly engage, and that it is easier to explain some passages in terms of the paranormal rather than the supernatural or the mythical. But that does not mean that all Gospel passages are to be regarded as historical; it may be that, while some phenomena will be accepted as paranormal, other passages will be regarded as natural events, and that the Evangelists themselves in some cases have heightened the effect of the stories that they tell by adding a phrase which I have regarded as indicating the paranormal.

At all times, the subject must be approached cautiously and rigorously. I have tried to give, where appropriate, examples from secular sources of comparable paranormal events or phenomena. These examples may seem trivial compared with the Gospel passages, but I have included them to show that the phenomena falling into these categories have a paranormal source rather than a supernatural origin, and, at the least, offer new insights into the ways we interpret a number of Gospel texts.

I do not expect my explanations in terms of the paranormal to be easily accepted. After all, this is (to the best of my knowledge) the first attempt in New Testament scholarship to use the category of the paranormal to interpret passages in the Gospels. Such a radical move is most unlikely to gain instant acceptance – the very idea certainly needs to be explored and investigated far more widely. I put forward this type of explanation as a fresh possibility to be considered. It is perhaps most likely to commend itself to those who believe that the Gospels are based on historical events and actual sayings, but who find it difficult to accept in many cases a miraculous or supernatural explanation. That is my own personal view. But there is no hidden agenda here: this study is not written in order to further any particular christological viewpoint and stands or falls on its premises and on its argumentation.

References

Beloff, J., *Parapsychology* (London: Athlone, 1993)

Boobyer, G. H., *St Mark and the Transfiguration Story* (Edinburgh: T. & T. Clark, 1942)

Borg, M. J., 'The Historical Study of Jesus and Christian Origins', in *Jesus at 2000*, ed. M. J. Borg (Boulder, CO: Westview Press, 1997)

Bruce, A. B., *The Miraculous Element in the Gospels* (London: Hodder & Stoughton, 1890)

Bultmann, R., *Die Geschichte der Synoptischen Tradition*, 2nd edn (Göttingen: Vandenhoeck & Ruprecht, 1931)

Bultmann, R., *The Gospel of John*, ET (Oxford: Blackwell, 1971)

Cadoux, C. J., *The Historic Mission of Jesus* (London: Lutterworth Press, 1941)

Caird, G. B., *The Gospel of St Luke* (Harmondsworth: Penguin, 1963)

Chadwick, H., *The Church in Ancient Society* (Oxford, 2001)

Charles, R., *Pseudepigrapha* (Oxford: Oxford University Press, 1913)

Cornwell, J., *Powers of Darkness, Powers of Light* (London: Viking, 1991)

Creed, J. M., *The Gospel According to St Luke* (London: Macmillan, 1942)

Crossan, M. J., *The Historical Jesus* (Edinburgh: T. & T. Clark, 1991)

Dawkins, R., *Unweaving the Rainbow* (London: Allen Lane, 1998)

Dibelius, M., *From Tradition to Gospel*, trs. B. L. Woolf (London: Macmillan, 1934)

Dodd, C. H., 'The Appearances of the Risen Christ', in *Studies in the Gospels*, ed. D. E. Nineham (Oxford: Blackwell, 1955)

Dodd, C. H., *Historical Tradition in the Fourth Gospel* (Cambridge: Cambridge University Press, 1963)

Eels, C. P., 'Life and Times of Apollonius of Tyana', *Stanford University Review*, 1923

Emmet, C. W., 'Loisy's View of the Resurrection', *Contemporary Review*, Vol. 96, 1909, pp. 588–99

Enright, D. J., *The Oxford Book of the Supernatural* (Oxford: Oxford University Press, 1995)

Eusebius, *Ecclesiastical History*

Fuller, R. H., 'Forgery, Interpretation or Old Tradition', *Colloquy*, Vol. 18 (Berkeley, CA: Centre for Hermeneutical Studies, 1975)

Gurney, E., Myers, F. W. H., and Podmore, F., 'On Apparitions Occurring Soon After Death', *Proceedings of the Society for Psychical Research* (London, 1989)

Gurney, E., Myers, F. W. H. and Podmore, F., *Phantasms of the Living* (London: Kegan Paul, 1918)

Hearne, K., *Visions of the Future* (Wellingborough: Aquarian, 1989)

Hume, D., *An Enquiry Concerning Human Understanding* (Oxford: Clarendon Press, 1902)

Josephus, *Antiquities of the Jews*

Koenig, H. G., McCullough, M. E., and Larson, P. B., *Handbook of Religion and Health* (Oxford: Oxford University Press, 2001)

Lake, K., *The Historical Evidence for the Resurrection of Jesus Christ* (London: Williams & Norgate, 1907)

Lambertini, P., *De Beatificatione et Canonizatione* (Venice, 1766)

Lemoyne, G. B., *Vita de B Giovanni Bosco* (published in Italian in 20 volumes, n.d.), Vol. 2, pp. 259–60

Macaffery, J., *The Friar of San Giovanni* (London: Darton, Longman & Todd, 1978)

Mackenzie, A. C., *Hauntings and Apparitions* (London: SPR/Heinemann, 1982)

Manning, M., *The Link* (Gerrards Cross: Smythe, 1974)

Manning, M., *One Foot in the Stars* (Shaftesbury: Element, 1999)

Meier, J., *A Marginal Jew*, 2 vols (New York: Doubleday, 1991)

Montefiore, H., 'Revolt in the Desert?', *Novum Testamentum*, Vol. 8, 1962, pp. 135–41

Montefiore, H., *The Paranormal: A Bishop Investigates* (Leicester: Upfront, 2002)

Montefiore, H., *The Womb and the Tomb* (London: Fount, 1992)

Morris, R., 'What Parapsychologists Do', *The Christian Parapsychologist*, December 2000, pp. 110f.

Myers, F. W. H., *Human Personality and its Survival of Bodily Death* (abridged) (London: Longmans, 1919)

Nineham, D. E., *The Gospel of St Mark* (Harmondsworth: Penguin, 1963)

Parnia, S., Waller, D. G., Yeates, R., and Fenwick, P., 'A Qualitative and Quantitive Study of the Incidence, Features and Aetiology of Near Death Experiences in Near Death Experiences', *Resuscitation*, Vol. 46, 2001

Perry, M. C., *The Easter Enigma* (London: Faber, 1959)

Pines, S., *An Arabic Version of the Testimonium Flavianum and its Implications* (Jerusalem: Israel Academy of Sciences and Humanities, 1971)

Ramsey, A. M., *The Glory of God and the Transfiguration of Christ* (London: Longmans, Green & Co., 1949)

Raudive, K., *Breakthrough* (Gerrards Cross: Smythe, 1971)

Rawlinson, A. E. J., *The Gospel According to St Mark* (London: Methuen, 1949)

Renan, E., *La Vie de Jesus* (Paris: Michel Levy Frères, 1863)

Richardson, A., *The Miracle Stories of the Gospels* (London: SCM, 1941)

Robinson, J. A. T., *The Priority of John* (London: SCM, 1985)

Salter, H. W., *Ghosts and Apparitions* (London: G. Bell & Sons, 1938)

Sanders, J. N., *A Commentary on the Gospel According to St John* (London: A. & C. Black, 1968)

Schweitzer, A., *The Quest for the Historical Jesus*, ET (London, 1949)

Scole Report, *Proceedings of the Society for Psychical Research* 58, 1999

Scully, V. (trs.), Thomas à Kempis, *St Lydwina of Schiedam* (1912)

Sheldrake, R., *The Sense of Being Stared At and Other Aspects of the Extended Mind* (London: Hutchinson, 2003)

Smith, M., *Clement of Alexandria and the Secret Gospel of Mark* (Cambridge, MA: Harvard University Press, 1973)

Smith, M., *Jesus the Magician* (Wellingborough: Aquarian, 1985)

Spong, J. S., *Born of a Woman* (New York: HarperSanFrancisco, 1992)

Stevenson, I., *Children Who Remember Previous Lives* (Charlottesville, VA: University Press of Virginia, 1987)

Stevenson, I., *European Cases of the Reincarnation Type* (Jefferson, NC: McFarland, 2003)

Streeter, B. H., *Foundations* (London: Macmillan, 1912)

Taylor, V., *The Gospel According to St Mark* (London: Macmillan, 1952)

Temple, W., *Nature, Man and God* (London: Macmillan, 1934)

Thompson, J. M., *Miracles in the New Testament* (London: Edward Arnold, 1911)

Thurston, H., *The Physical Phenomena of Mysticism* (London: Burns & Oates, 1952)

Tyrrell, G. N. M., *Apparitions* (London: Duckworth, 1953)

Tyrrell, G. N. M., *The Personality of Man* (West Drayton: Penguin, 1947)

Underhill, E., *The Mystic Way* (London: Dent, 1913)

Vermes, G., *Jesus the Jew* (London: SCM, 1974)

Wellhausen, J., *Das Evangelium Marci*, 7th edn (Berlin, 1909)

Wiebe, P. H., *The Visions of Jesus*, (New York and Oxford: Oxford University Press, 1997)

Wiles, M., *The Remaking of Christian Doctrine* (London: SCM, 1974)

Woods, G. F., 'The Evidential Value of Biblical Miracles', in *Miracles*, ed. C. F. D. Moule (London: Mowbray, 1965)

Zeki, S., *A Vision of the Brain* (Oxford: Blackwell, 1993)